CAREERS
AND
CHAOS

Henry Blackwell is a workplace futurist, career strategist, and bestselling author of Workshift. With roots in corporate consulting and a reputation for decoding tectonic shifts in the economy, Henry has advised Fortune 500 leaders, startup founders, and solo entrepreneurs on how to pivot, adapt, and thrive in an era where disruption is the norm. His work blends sharp analysis with real-world grit, drawing on interviews, trends, and his career reinventions. *Careers and Chaos* delivers a frank roadmap for navigating uncertainty—with hustle, clarity, and nerve. When he's not researching the future of work, Henry mentors first-generation entrepreneurs and guest lectures on adaptive strategy at leading business schools.

CAREERS AND CHAOS

THRIVING IN THE ERA OF **AI**, **LAYOFFS** AND **SIDE HUSTLES**

HENRY BLACKWELL

RUPA

Published by
Rupa Publications India Pvt. Ltd 2025
161-B/4, Gulmohar House,
Yusuf Sarai Community Centre,
New Delhi 110049

Sales centres:
Bengaluru Chennai
Hyderabad Kolkata Mumbai

Edition Copyright © Rupa Publications India Pvt. Ltd 2025

The views and opinions expressed in this book are the
author's own and the facts are as reported by him which
have been verified to the extent possible, and the publishers
are not in any way liable for the same.

P-ISBN: 978-93-7003-506-5
E-ISBN: 978-93-7003-043-5

First impression 2025

10 9 8 7 6 5 4 3 2 1

The moral right of the author has been asserted

Printed in India

Contents

PART 1

The Career Playbook Is Dead—Rewrite the Rules

1

Your Dream Job Is a Myth (And That's a Good Thing)

FOR YEARS, WE'VE BEEN SOLD a shiny, one-size-fits-all fantasy: find your "dream job," work hard, climb the ladder, and everything will magically fall into place. It's a comforting narrative—a linear path where ambition meets security. The problem? That world doesn't exist anymore. The career playbook your parents followed is outdated, and the so-called dream job is nothing more than a marketing myth designed to keep you chasing a goalpost that moves every time you get closer. And maybe—just maybe—that's a good thing.

Let's break it down: the idea of a "dream job" suggests there's one perfect position out there that will fulfill every aspiration, pay you what you're worth, and offer a sense of purpose. But the modern economy doesn't work like that. Jobs are more disposable than ever, industries are evolving at breakneck speed, and the skills that got you hired yesterday might be obsolete tomorrow. Pinning your happiness and self-worth to a singular role is a risky bet in a world that's constantly shifting. And truthfully? It's a bet most people lose.

The rise of artificial intelligence, automation, and global competition has made traditional career paths less predictable—

and less promising. No company is offering lifelong security, and no position is immune to disruption. The layoffs that once seemed like a distant threat are now a regular headline. The workforce has changed, and if you're still clinging to the belief that a dream job will solve all your problems, you're playing a losing game.

But here's where things get interesting. When you stop chasing the illusion of a perfect job, you open yourself up to something far more powerful—freedom. When you realize no employer holds the key to your happiness or financial future, you gain the power to design a career on your own terms. It's no longer about fitting into someone else's box. It's about building a life where your work adapts to your ambitions, not the other way around.

Flexibility is the new currency. The people thriving in today's economy aren't the ones clinging to one job title or industry—they're the ones who pivot. They know how to acquire new skills, spot emerging opportunities, and diversify their income streams. The old model of corporate loyalty rewarded years of service with predictable promotions. Today, loyalty to a single employer often leads to stagnation, while those who embrace agility are the ones who stay ahead. Companies no longer view employees as family—they view them as assets. And the minute you stop generating value, you're expendable. Harsh? Maybe. But once you accept that reality, you can start playing the game on your own terms.

The danger of tying your identity to a job title is that it makes you vulnerable. When your sense of self is wrapped up in a specific role or career path, any disruption—whether it's a layoff, a toxic work environment, or a sudden industry shift—can feel like a personal failure. But your worth isn't defined by what you do for a living. You are not your job. And when you unhook your identity from a title, you give yourself permission to explore new paths without feeling like you're betraying some outdated vision of success.

Think about it—how many people do you know who landed their so-called dream job only to realize it didn't deliver the happiness or freedom they expected? The truth is, no single job can meet every need. It's not about finding one role that fulfills you; it's about crafting a career ecosystem that supports your life. This means embracing a mindset where change isn't a threat—it's an opportunity.

In the current landscape, career security comes from adaptability, not tenure. The most valuable skill you can develop is the ability to reinvent yourself. Instead of chasing a singular dream job, focus on acquiring high-value skills that travel across industries. Become the kind of person who can thrive in any environment, whether you're working a traditional role, freelancing, or launching a side hustle. The people who win today aren't the ones clinging to stability—they're the ones who stay fluid.

And here's the kicker: the death of the dream job means you're no longer trapped in someone else's definition of success. For decades, we were told that climbing the corporate ladder was the pinnacle of achievement. But what if you don't want to climb? What if you want to build something of your own? What if you want the freedom to explore multiple passions instead of locking yourself into one path? When you abandon the fantasy of a singular dream job, you give yourself permission to pursue a more expansive vision for your life—one where work fits around your values, not the other way around.

This isn't about rejecting ambition—it's about redefining it. Ambition today doesn't mean grinding for one employer for 40 years. It means creating options. It means having the skills and leverage to walk away from situations that no longer serve you. It means building a life where your work supports your goals without consuming your identity. And that kind of freedom is worth far more than any job title.

So, what does this look like in practice? It starts with questioning the assumptions you've been handed. Instead of asking, "What's my dream job?" ask yourself, "What kind of life do I want to build?" Do you want autonomy? Financial independence? Creative fulfillment? Once you define what matters most, you can reverse-engineer a career that delivers those outcomes—without being limited by traditional paths.

It also means adopting a portfolio mindset. In a world where no job is guaranteed, the smartest move is to diversify your professional identity. This could mean building a side hustle while working a 9-to-5, developing passive income streams, or acquiring skills that open up new opportunities. You're not just one thing—you're a multidimensional person with a range of talents. Embrace that. Explore that. Profit from that.

And perhaps most importantly, let go of the pressure to have it all figured out. Careers are no longer linear, and there's no single path to success. What works today might not work tomorrow—and that's okay. The people who thrive in the chaos aren't the ones with rigid five-year plans. They're the ones who stay curious, stay adaptable, and know when it's time to pivot. Success isn't about landing one perfect job—it's about building a life where you get to call the shots.

The dream job is a myth. But when you release that myth, you gain something far more valuable—freedom. The freedom to explore, to evolve, and to craft a career that aligns with the life you actually want to live. In a world where nothing is promised, that kind of freedom isn't just a luxury—it's a necessity.

2

AI Isn't Taking Over—But It's Changing Everything

THE FEAR OF ARTIFICIAL INTELLIGENCE replacing human jobs isn't new—but lately, it's louder than ever. Every headline screams that the robots are coming, entire industries are bracing for automation, and it's easy to feel like you're one algorithm away from being obsolete. But here's the truth: AI isn't here to take your job—it's here to change the way you work. And if you know how to move with the shift instead of against it, you're not just safe—you're ahead of the game.

The panic around AI taking over stems from a fundamental misunderstanding of what technology can and can't do. Sure, AI is getting smarter, faster, and more efficient—but it still lacks the uniquely human qualities that make you invaluable. Creativity, emotional intelligence, critical thinking—these are the tools that machines can't mimic, and they're becoming the currency of the future job market. So instead of asking, "Will AI replace me?" start asking, "How can I use AI to amplify my value?" Because the people who understand how to work with AI—rather than against it—are the ones who will thrive in this new landscape.

One of the biggest shifts AI is driving is how job descriptions are evolving. Tasks that were once human-only—data entry, scheduling, even basic content creation—are now automated. But that doesn't mean your job disappears; it means your role expands. Repetitive work is being handed off to machines, leaving you with more room to focus on the things AI can't do—like making strategic decisions, solving complex problems, and building genuine human relationships. If you're stuck in the mindset that your value lies in performing routine tasks, AI will feel like a threat. But if you see yourself as someone who thinks, leads, and innovates, AI becomes a tool—not a competitor.

Think of it this way: AI is the assistant, not the CEO. It can handle the mechanics, but it can't replace vision. And in today's economy, the people who bring vision to the table are the ones who shape industries. If you can master the art of using AI to streamline the "busy work," you create space to focus on higher-level contributions that machines simply can't replicate. That's not just job security—that's leverage.

Of course, not all industries are affected equally. The fields most vulnerable to automation tend to rely on repetitive, rule-based processes. Data analysis, customer support, and administrative roles are all being redefined by technology. But if you're in a field where creativity, empathy, or nuanced decision-making is key, your job is safer—at least for now. Healthcare professionals, educators, and creative leaders are harder to replace because their work involves human complexity. That doesn't mean you're immune—but it does mean that leaning into the human side of your skills will make you more irreplaceable.

The real risk isn't AI itself—it's being unprepared for the ways AI is reshaping the job market. If you're standing still while technology advances, you're playing a dangerous game. But if you're willing to evolve, you have the upper hand. This is why future-proofing your career is about focusing on what AI *can't* do.

Machines can analyze data—but they can't interpret the emotional context behind it. They can produce words—but they can't tell stories that stir the human soul. They can identify patterns—but they can't dream, invent, or imagine beyond those patterns. And that's where you come in.

To stay ahead, you need to prioritize skills that are inherently human. Creativity isn't just for artists—it's a competitive advantage. Critical thinking—the ability to question assumptions and solve problems in new ways—is more valuable than ever. Emotional intelligence—the ability to understand and respond to human emotions—remains unmatched by machines. And adaptability— the willingness to learn, pivot, and grow—is becoming the single most important skill of the digital age. AI isn't static. Neither should you be.

But it's not just about protecting yourself—it's about leveraging AI to unlock new opportunities. Those who thrive in this new world will be the ones who treat AI as a collaborator, not a competitor. Learning how to integrate AI into your workflow allows you to work smarter, not harder. Tools like ChatGPT, Midjourney, and automation software aren't just novelties— they're accelerators. If you're using them to cut down on time-consuming tasks, you free up bandwidth for deeper, more strategic work. And that's where real value is created.

Consider the new career landscape: marketers who use AI to analyze consumer behavior can craft sharper, more personalized campaigns. Writers who use AI for research can focus on creating narratives that engage and inspire. Entrepreneurs who automate administrative tasks can spend more time building relationships and expanding their vision. The people who win aren't the ones who reject AI—they're the ones who integrate it seamlessly into their skillset.

And here's the kicker: tech literacy is no longer optional. Whether you're in finance, fashion, or freelance work, understanding how AI operates is now part of the baseline. You don't need to be a programmer—but you do need to know how to navigate the tools that are reshaping every industry. If you're not actively learning how to work with these systems, you're falling behind. But if you stay curious and keep evolving, you position yourself as someone who doesn't just survive the shift— you drive it.

The bottom line? AI isn't here to steal your career—it's here to redefine it. And in many ways, that's a gift. Because when the machines take over the mundane, you're left with the space to do the work that actually matters. You're not just an employee— you're a strategist, a visionary, a creator. The people who get that— who lean into their human edge while mastering the tech—are the ones who will shape the future.

The age of AI isn't a death sentence for your career. It's an invitation to rise, to evolve, and to own your place in a world that's being rebuilt in real-time. But here's the catch—you have to move. The world isn't waiting, and the people who cling to the old ways will be left behind. If you want to future-proof your career, it's time to stop fearing AI and start leading with the things that make you impossible to replace. The machines are here—but so are you. And no algorithm can do what you do when you step into your full power.

3

Layoffs Are the New Normal— Here's How to Stay Ready

EARLIER IN THE DAY, A "secure job" meant a steady paycheck, annual raises, and the golden promise of retiring with a fat pension. Those days? Gone. In today's economy, layoffs aren't rare—they're routine. Companies slash workforces not just during recessions but as part of their quarterly strategy. One minute you're updating your LinkedIn bio with a shiny new title, and the next, you're holding a cardboard box while HR explains severance packages. The harsh truth? No job is bulletproof. But here's the upside: if you know how to stay ready, you'll never be caught off guard.

The first rule of surviving layoff culture is recognizing the signs before the axe falls. Companies rarely wake up and decide to fire half the workforce overnight. There are always breadcrumbs— if you know where to look. Are budgets getting tighter? Are projects being canceled without clear explanations? Are executives suddenly obsessed with "efficiency" and "streamlining processes"? These aren't just buzzwords—they're warning bells. If senior leaders are dropping phrases like "right-sizing" or "workforce optimization," you'd better believe layoffs are on the horizon.

Another red flag? Hiring freezes. When a company stops

bringing in new talent, it's a sure sign they're bracing for cuts. Pay attention to how leadership communicates—vague, overly positive messaging often masks deeper problems. If the town hall meetings suddenly sound like a TED Talk on resilience and agility, it's time to update your résumé. And don't ignore subtle shifts in your daily workload. If responsibilities are being quietly redistributed, someone's about to get the boot—and you don't want it to be you.

But knowing the signs isn't enough. You need to be ready *before* the pink slip arrives. Waiting until you're laid off to prepare is like building a life raft after the ship starts sinking. Smart professionals treat job security as a moving target—not a guarantee. This means keeping your professional toolkit sharp and your network even sharper. Update your résumé regularly— don't wait until you're scrambling. Keep a running list of your achievements, quantifiable wins, and projects that showcase your value. When the time comes, you won't be rewriting your career story—you'll be ready to tell it.

Networking isn't just for extroverts in tailored blazers—it's your best insurance policy against career disruption. Don't wait until you need a job to start connecting. Nurture relationships while you're still employed. Attend industry events, join digital communities, and engage on professional platforms like LinkedIn. Your network is more than a collection of contacts—it's your safety net. When layoffs hit, the people who've invested in genuine connections rebound the fastest. If you disappear into your cubicle and resurface only when you need help, you've already lost.

And while you're employed, build an emergency fund like your future depends on it—because it does. Conventional wisdom says three to six months' worth of expenses is the goal. In reality? Aim higher. Layoffs can drag out longer than expected, and severance packages (if you're lucky enough to get one) won't last forever. Financial flexibility gives you breathing room to make your next move strategically, not out of desperation.

So, what happens if the worst-case scenario hits? First, breathe. Panic is the enemy of progress. The moment you get laid off, prioritize your immediate needs. Request your severance package details in writing, including unused vacation pay, health benefits, and any outplacement support. If the paperwork feels confusing or incomplete, don't be afraid to ask questions—or consult a lawyer if necessary. This isn't just about fairness—it's about securing every dollar you're owed.

Next, file for unemployment benefits as soon as possible. There's no shame in using resources designed to support you during transition periods. Delaying this step only makes the financial strain worse. Then, update your professional profiles—especially LinkedIn—with a focus on your skills and achievements, not your job loss. The way you frame your narrative matters. You didn't "get laid off"—your role was eliminated, and now you're available for new opportunities. The right language signals resilience and professionalism, not defeat.

Once you've handled logistics, it's time to activate your network. Let trusted contacts know you're on the market. Be specific—don't just say you're "open to opportunities." Clearly outline the roles you want, the industries you're targeting, and the value you bring. People want to help, but you need to make it easy for them. And don't overlook the power of "weak ties." Sometimes the best opportunities come from acquaintances rather than close friends, because they move in circles you don't.

Job loss can feel personal—but it's not. Layoffs are business decisions, not value judgments. The faster you separate your self-worth from your job title, the faster you'll bounce back. Instead of spiraling, treat this moment as an inflection point—a chance to reevaluate where you want to go next. Is there a skill you've been meaning to learn? A career pivot you've been craving? Use this period to take bold steps toward the future you actually want.

And here's the kicker—job security no longer comes from a single employer. It comes from having an exit plan at all times. Even if you love your current role, assume nothing is permanent. Keep side projects alive. Explore freelance gigs. Diversify your income streams wherever possible. If your entire livelihood depends on one paycheck, you're walking a tightrope without a safety net. The new era of career stability is about optionality—the freedom to choose your next move before anyone else decides it for you.

The world of work is shifting fast, and layoffs are no longer the exception—they're the norm. But this doesn't have to be a death sentence for your career. The people who thrive aren't the ones clinging to outdated ideas of job security—they're the ones who stay agile, stay prepared, and always have a Plan B (and C). If you're proactive instead of reactive, no layoff can break you. In fact, it might just be the launchpad for something better.

So, here's your reality check: no job is guaranteed—but your readiness is. Stay sharp, stay connected, and always be ready to make your next move—because in this economy, staying ready is the only real security left.

4

Résumés Are Out—Your Digital Presence Is In

ONCE UPON A TIME, A polished résumé printed on crisp white paper was your golden ticket to career success. It was your entire professional identity condensed onto a page—maybe two if you were bold. But in today's hyper-connected world, that piece of paper is about as relevant as a fax machine. Employers aren't just skimming bullet points on a static document anymore—they're Googling you. They're scrolling through your LinkedIn, lurking on your social media, and making snap decisions about your value before you even step into an interview. In the digital age, your online presence isn't just part of the hiring process—it *is* the hiring process.

Let's get real: recruiters are busy. They aren't spending hours dissecting résumés like forensic scientists. Instead, they're scanning digital profiles in seconds. And while you're busy formatting your work history into neat little bullet points, your next job offer could be slipping through the cracks because your online presence isn't doing the heavy lifting. If your LinkedIn looks like an afterthought or your Google search results are a ghost town, you're already behind.

Think of LinkedIn as your new résumé—but with better

lighting and 24/7 accessibility. It's not just a professional networking site anymore—it's a dynamic, real-time career billboard that's working for you while you sleep. A bare-bones profile with a blurry profile picture and a vague job title won't cut it. Your headline isn't just a job description—it's a mini elevator pitch. Are you a "Marketing Manager," or are you "Driving Revenue Growth Through Data-Driven Marketing Strategies"? One tells people what you do. The other tells them why you're valuable.

Your *About* section? It's not the place to regurgitate your job duties. It's your opportunity to tell your career story—why you do what you do and how you do it better than anyone else. This is where you flex your impact. Don't just say you "led projects." Talk about the multi-million-pound campaign you spearheaded or the processes you transformed. Metrics matter. Numbers stand out. Specificity wins. And while you're at it, make sure your skills section is stacked and endorsed—because, yes, recruiters are filtering candidates by keywords, and if your profile is thin, you're invisible.

But LinkedIn is just the beginning. If you want to future-proof your career, you need to extend your digital footprint beyond a corporate platform. A personal website is no longer optional—it's your secret weapon. Imagine a space that's 100% under your control. No algorithms. No platform rules. Just you, showcasing your expertise on your terms. Whether you're a creative professional sharing a portfolio, a consultant highlighting case studies, or a tech wizard documenting your latest innovations, a website signals one thing clearly: you're serious. And it's not just about showing off—it's about discoverability. A well-optimized site means when someone Googles you, they find a curated, intentional snapshot of your career—not random tweets from 2012.

If building a website sounds like a massive undertaking, breathe. You don't need to code or spend thousands on a designer. Platforms like Squarespace, Wix, and WordPress have made it easier than ever to create sleek, professional sites in a matter of hours. At minimum, your site should include a bio, your work highlights, and clear ways to contact you. Bonus points if you add thought leadership—original articles, project breakdowns, or even a blog. The goal isn't perfection—it's visibility.

And here's something most people overlook: personal branding isn't just for influencers. It's your career insurance policy. Whether you realize it or not, you already have a personal brand—the question is whether you're actively shaping it or letting the internet do it for you. What do you want to be known for? What problems do you solve better than anyone else? When someone hears your name in a meeting, what's the first thing that comes to mind? If you're not defining your narrative, someone else will—and they probably won't get it right.

Visibility isn't vanity—it's currency. The more strategically visible you are, the more opportunities will come your way. But here's the key: be intentional. Posting random career updates once a year won't cut it. Share insights that showcase your expertise. Engage with industry conversations. If you've achieved something remarkable, talk about it. The internet moves fast, and if you're not actively contributing to the dialogue, you're disappearing from it.

And don't sleep on search engine optimization (SEO). Yes, even for your career. Recruiters are typing specific phrases into search bars right now. If your digital presence isn't optimized for those terms, you won't show up. If you're a UX designer, are you describing yourself that way across platforms? If you specialize in fintech law, is that keyword woven into your LinkedIn summary? The digital world doesn't reward humility—it rewards clarity.

Make it easy for people to find you, understand you, and hire you.

But maybe you're wondering—if I'm not looking for a new job, does this really matter? Absolutely. Career stability no longer comes from job titles or tenure—it comes from options. And the best way to create options is to become a magnet for opportunities. When you build a strong digital brand, you stop chasing jobs and start attracting them. You become the person people think of when they have a role to fill, a problem to solve, or a panel to invite a speaker to. Opportunities don't just fall from the sky—they find the people who've made themselves visible.

And let's be honest—résumés feel one-dimensional because they *are*. They reduce your career to bullet points and jargon. Your digital presence, on the other hand, is expansive. It tells the full, dynamic story of who you are and where you're going. It gives you a voice in your industry, a platform to showcase your talents, and a competitive edge in a market where standing out isn't optional—it's survival.

In a world where algorithms decide whose profiles get seen and which candidates get shortlisted, relying on a paper résumé is like bringing a knife to a tech fight. The future belongs to those who embrace the digital stage—not those clinging to outdated career traditions.

So, what's the move? Start where you are, but don't stay there. Audit your digital presence regularly. Optimize your profiles. Build a space that reflects your best work. And remember—your next career move might not come from a job board. It could be one search, one click, one digital impression away. If you're not showing up online, you're not showing up at all.

5

Job Security Is a Lie—Skills Are Your Real Safety Net

FOR DECADES, THE PROMISE WAS simple: get a stable job, stay loyal, and the company will take care of you. Pensions, promotions, and predictable career paths were the reward for playing by the rules. But that promise? It's dead. The truth is, no job is truly secure—not when industries are being upended by technology, globalization, and economic shifts. What protects you isn't a fancy job title or how long you've clocked in at one company. It's your skills—the real currency in a world where entire roles can disappear overnight.

Consider this: millions of jobs that existed a decade ago no longer do. Typists, switchboard operators, and DVD store clerks? Gone. And while new roles like UX designers, AI ethicists, and digital marketers have emerged, the speed of change hasn't slowed down. If you're banking on job security in this environment, you're already behind. What you need is *skill security*—a constantly evolving toolkit that ensures you remain valuable no matter how industries shift.

The first lie you need to unlearn is that a job title equals safety. Titles are static; skills are dynamic. Being a "Marketing Manager" or "Project Lead" sounds impressive until your company gets acquired, restructured, or automated. What actually keeps you employed—and employable—are the specific, transferable skills behind those titles. Can you analyze data? Solve complex problems? Communicate ideas clearly across platforms? These are the capabilities that transcend job descriptions and make you indispensable.

So, what are the skills that guarantee future opportunities? They aren't just technical—although tech literacy is non-negotiable in today's economy. It's a blend of what machines can't do and what businesses will always need. Critical thinking, creativity, emotional intelligence, and adaptability top the list. You could call them "soft skills," but there's nothing soft about the advantage they give you. Meanwhile, hard skills like coding, digital marketing, and data analysis continue to dominate hiring trends. But the real power move? Combining both. If you can blend technical expertise with human-centric skills, you become irreplaceable.

But here's the good news—you don't need to spend years in a classroom to stay relevant. Learning today is faster, cheaper, and more accessible than ever. Forget the traditional degree path if it no longer fits your life. Micro-credentials, online courses, and self-directed learning offer an edge without the time and cost of another degree. Platforms like Coursera, LinkedIn Learning, and YouTube University (yes, it counts) are goldmines for people who want to level up on their own terms. The real flex is learning continuously—not waiting for your employer to train you.

The smartest career move you can make is building a *skills portfolio*—a tangible collection of what you know and can do. It's not just a résumé; it's living proof of your expertise. This might mean a GitHub repository showcasing your coding projects, a Medium page full of thought leadership articles, or a portfolio website that highlights case studies. When layoffs hit or a recruiter comes knocking, you won't just have a job title—you'll have a body of work that speaks for itself.

And don't make the mistake of locking your skills into one industry. Specialization is important, but versatility is what future-proofs you. Think about it—AI won't just change tech jobs. It's already transforming healthcare, finance, media, and beyond. The skills you sharpen in one sector could open doors in another if you're paying attention. If you can manage projects, lead teams, or interpret complex data, those skills are valuable everywhere.

What separates people who thrive in uncertain economies from those who struggle is their ability to adapt. And adaptability isn't some vague buzzword—it's a skill in itself. It's the ability to stay curious, learn on the fly, and pivot when the market demands it. It means recognizing when your industry is shifting and making proactive moves instead of waiting to be forced into change. Those who embrace a growth mindset—the belief that your abilities can be developed through effort and learning—consistently outperform those clinging to old paradigms.

Still, you might be thinking—what if I'm already comfortable? What if my job feels secure? The harsh truth is, comfort is a trap. The companies you work for will do what's best for their bottom line, and you are not immune. The moment you assume your role is untouchable is the moment you become vulnerable. You owe it to yourself to be future-ready. That means keeping a pulse on emerging trends, regularly auditing your skills, and committing to lifelong learning.

Staying ahead doesn't require predicting the future—it requires preparing for multiple futures. Start by identifying your core strengths and the gaps in your skillset. What's in demand right now? What's likely to grow in value? If you're in marketing, learn data analytics. If you're in operations, get familiar with

AI-driven workflows. No matter your field, communication and problem-solving will never go out of style. And here's a game-changer: develop skills that monetize outside your 9-to-5. Being able to generate income beyond a paycheck isn't just a side hustle—it's a safety net.

And let's talk about leverage. When you have a deep, versatile skillset, you have bargaining power. You're not at the mercy of a single employer. You can negotiate better salaries, seek remote work options, or transition into consulting. Skills give you the freedom to shape your career on your terms.

Ultimately, job security is a comforting illusion in a world that changes by the minute. The only real security is your ability to stay valuable—no matter where you work, who you work for, or how industries evolve. So, stop chasing stability through outdated career myths. Invest in your skills. Build a portfolio that showcases your expertise. And stay agile, because the future belongs to those who refuse to stand still.

The lesson is clear: You are not your job title. You are the sum of your skills. And in a world where nothing is guaranteed, that's the closest thing to security you'll ever have.

PART 2

Hustle Smarter—Because One Paycheck Won't Cut It

6

Why a 9-to-5 Is Just One Piece of the Puzzle

FOR GENERATIONS, THE 9-TO-5 WAS sold as the ultimate goal. Get a job, work hard, and climb the ladder—that's how you "made it." But let's be honest: that dream expired the moment companies started laying off loyal employees with no warning, cost of living skyrocketed, and a single paycheck no longer covered the basics. The truth? Depending on one job in today's world is like walking a financial tightrope—one shake, and everything can fall apart.

The hidden risks of relying on a single income stream are bigger than most people realize. For starters, job security is more fragile than ever. Even the most "stable" industries are vulnerable to economic shifts, automation, and corporate restructuring. No matter how good you are at your job, decisions about your employment are often made in boardrooms you're not invited to. One layoff notice can turn a comfortable life into a financial nightmare—unless you've got backup. And it's not just job loss that's risky. When all your money flows from one source, you're stuck playing by someone else's rules—when to work, how much you earn, and even how much time you can take off. That's not freedom; that's a trap.

But here's the flip side: multi-income professionals don't

just survive these shifts—they thrive. Having multiple streams of income means you're no longer chained to one employer's whims. If one source dries up, you've got others keeping you afloat. And it's not just about financial safety—it's about options. Want to take a break without draining your savings? Extra income makes that possible. Dream of leaving a toxic work environment? A side hustle gives you an exit plan. When your income comes from different places, you get to call more shots. You become harder to break because no one person or company holds all the power.

And let's not ignore the fun factor. Diversifying your income can bring back the spark that a traditional 9-to-5 often kills. Maybe your job pays the bills but doesn't fulfill you creatively. A side hustle can be your outlet—whether it's starting a podcast, running a niche online store, or freelancing your skills. You get to explore new interests while building extra cash flow. Plus, multiple income streams give you access to experiences that a single paycheck often can't—travel, hobbies, and the ability to invest in your passions without stressing over money.

The best part? You don't have to quit your job to build these extra layers of income. The idea isn't to burn everything down—it's to create financial flexibility while keeping the stability you already have. It's about working smarter, not harder. The key is to find low-lift, high-reward opportunities that fit into your life. Think of it like stacking Legos—each piece adds strength without dismantling what's already built. For some, this means monetizing skills they already have. Are you a writer, designer, or analyst? Freelance it. Others may lean into digital products— ebooks, online courses, or templates that generate passive income. If you love sharing knowledge, coaching or consulting can be a lucrative add-on. And if you want money working for you, investments—whether in the stock market, real estate, or peer-to-peer lending—are powerful tools for multiplying your cash.

Of course, the biggest fear people have is burnout. And fair—it's a real risk if you try to do too much at once. The secret is balance. Don't jump into every opportunity blindly. Instead, choose income streams that align with your skills and lifestyle. If you only have five hours a week, start small—one freelance project or one digital product. Automate where you can. Use tools that streamline the process, like scheduling software for service-based work or platforms like Etsy and Gumroad for passive sales. And remember: your 9-to-5 doesn't have to be the enemy. It can fund your side ventures while providing benefits like health insurance and retirement contributions. Think of your job as your financial foundation—while your other income streams expand your freedom.

But beyond the logistics, the most crucial shift you need is mental. Moving from employee to multi-hyphenate requires unlearning the old career script. You're not just a job title—you're a brand, a business, and an asset in the marketplace. This mindset change isn't just about making extra cash; it's about realizing you have more to offer than any job description can capture. Multi-income living means rejecting the "one path" myth and embracing a life where your talents, interests, and ambitions all have room to grow.

The world is evolving too fast for a single paycheck to keep up. Inflation, job market volatility, and rising living costs mean playing it safe isn't so safe anymore. The people who thrive in this new reality are the ones who diversify early—before they're forced to. Whether you want to cushion yourself against layoffs, create financial breathing room, or buy back your time, multiple income streams aren't a luxury—they're a necessity.

So, if you've been waiting for permission to think bigger—

here it is. You don't have to choose between a job and freedom. You can have both. Your 9-to-5 is just one piece of the puzzle—but you're the one holding all the other pieces. And when you start building beyond a single paycheck, you're not just surviving the chaos—you're owning it.

7

Side Hustles Aren't Optional— They're Survival

THE BELIEF THAT A FULL-TIME job is the ultimate symbol of stability is outdated and dangerous. For decades, people were taught that if you work hard, stay loyal to your employer, and follow the rules, you'll be rewarded with job security and a comfortable retirement. That promise no longer exists. In today's volatile job market—where layoffs are common, industries evolve overnight, and technology like AI is automating tasks—relying on a single paycheck is like playing financial Russian roulette. One unexpected pink slip, corporate merger, or economic downturn can wipe out your entire livelihood. That's why side hustles aren't just a trendy way to make extra cash—they're a necessary form of survival.

Let's be clear: no job is truly "safe." Even the most prestigious companies aren't immune to cuts. Google, Amazon, and other tech giants—once seen as the epitome of job security—routinely trim their workforces. And if major players aren't untouchable, neither are you. The gig economy is expanding while traditional employment shrinks. Workers across industries are realizing that a steady paycheck is anything but guaranteed. In this new reality, the smartest professionals are diversifying their income through side hustles—not because they want to, but because they have to.

Side hustles aren't just about making ends meet—they're about reclaiming power. When you rely solely on a corporate paycheck, you're always one decision away from financial disaster. But when you create independent income streams, you regain control. A side hustle can be a cushion when times get tough, a launchpad for new opportunities, or even an exit route from a soul-sucking job. In short, it's financial insurance in a world where loyalty means nothing, and layoffs are the norm.

But here's the thing: not all side hustles are created equal. There's a big difference between picking up a few extra gigs for fast cash and building a scalable, sustainable income stream. The former might pay the bills temporarily, but the latter changes your life. Smart side hustles work for you, even when you're not working. They generate revenue while you sleep, offer long-term growth, and eventually, give you the option to walk away from traditional employment altogether.

The first step in building a side hustle is to stop thinking small. Forget the cliché of driving for a rideshare app or filling out online surveys. While these activities may provide pocket change, they won't build lasting wealth or security. The real opportunity lies in leveraging your existing skills, knowledge, and experiences to create a business that grows. Think about what you already know—what can you monetize? Maybe you're an expert in a specific industry, a creative with marketable talents, or someone with the ability to teach others. Your expertise is more valuable than you realize, and there are people willing to pay for it.

Successful side hustlers treat their ventures like real businesses from day one. This means defining clear goals, understanding your market, and building systems to scale. One of the biggest mistakes people make is treating their side hustle like a hobby—

something they work on "when they have time." That mindset keeps you stuck. If you want a side hustle to transform your financial reality, you have to prioritize it. You schedule time for it the same way you would for a job because, eventually, it might become one.

A common barrier to starting a side hustle is time—or rather, the perceived lack of it. If you're already working full-time, where do you find the hours to build something new? The truth is, time isn't the problem—prioritization is. Everyone has the same 24 hours a day, but how you use them determines your outcomes. Successful side hustlers audit their schedules and identify "dead time"—those hours spent scrolling through social media, watching TV, or doing things that don't contribute to their goals. Reclaiming even a few hours a week is enough to start building a foundation. Consistency beats intensity. You don't need to spend ten hours a day grinding on your side hustle—you just need to show up regularly and do the work.

Your day job can also be a valuable resource for your side hustle—if you know how to use it. Many of the skills you use in your 9-to-5 are transferable. If you work in marketing, you already understand audience targeting. If you're in project management, you know how to organize tasks and workflows. Your employer is also funding your side hustle by providing the financial stability to experiment and invest. Don't view your job and your side hustle as competitors. They can coexist and even fuel each other—until you're ready to make the leap.

And here's an insider tip: you don't have to announce your side hustle to the world immediately. In fact, the early stages of building should be quiet and intentional. Work behind the scenes, refine your offering, and ensure it's generating consistent income before broadcasting your moves. Not every employer is thrilled about their employees having outside businesses, so being discreet protects both your job and your future hustle.

So, what happens when your side hustle gains momentum? At what point do you consider leaving your full-time job? The answer isn't as simple as matching your salary. Smart entrepreneurs understand that financial independence requires more than replacing a paycheck—it requires building a system that is both sustainable and scalable. The right time to transition is when your side hustle consistently covers your living expenses, provides a safety cushion, and shows clear growth potential. Walking away from a guaranteed paycheck is risky—but if your side hustle gives you freedom, control, and a bigger upside, the risk is worth taking.

But even if you never leave your day job, a side hustle still transforms your relationship with work. You're no longer beholden to a single employer. If you get laid off, you have a backup plan. If your boss overworks you, you can walk away with confidence. And if you want to pursue other dreams, your side hustle gives you the financial breathing room to do so. This isn't just about money—it's about autonomy. In a world where employers hold the cards, a side hustle puts some power back in your hands.

The best part? There's no "perfect" time to start. You don't need a massive investment, a fancy website, or the latest technology. You just need to begin. Start small, learn as you go, and scale up over time. Every empire starts with a single step, and your future is too valuable to leave in someone else's hands.

In this new economy, the rules have changed. Job security is a myth, and no one is coming to save you. But that's not a reason to panic—it's an invitation to take control. Side hustles aren't optional—they're a survival strategy for anyone who wants to thrive in an unpredictable world. Whether you're building a freelance business, launching a digital product, or creating a niche service, your side hustle is the key to financial freedom and future-proofing your career.

Because in the end, the only job security that exists is the security you create for yourself. And the sooner you start, the sooner you'll stop depending on anyone else to pay your bills.

8

Freelancing Looks Fun Until You're Doing It

ON THE SURFACE, FREELANCING LOOKS like the ultimate career glow-up. No boss breathing down your neck, no rigid schedules, and the freedom to work from a beach if you feel like it. It's the dream, right? That Instagram-perfect life where you answer emails in sweatpants and take mid-week vacations. But here's the truth: behind the glossy filters is a hustle most people aren't ready for. Freelancing is less about sipping lattes and more about chasing invoices, negotiating fees, and wondering if your next gig will cover the rent.

The first shock most freelancers face is how quickly freedom can feel like free-falling. When you leave a traditional job, you also leave behind predictable paychecks, employer-sponsored benefits, and the comfort of knowing where your next dollar is coming from. Suddenly, you're your own HR department, marketing team, and accountant—all while delivering work to clients who expect you to be available 24/7. And while it's true that you get to decide when and how you work, what no one tells you is that freedom comes with a heavy tax: instability.

The feast-or-famine cycle is real. One month, your inbox is overflowing with clients begging for your expertise; the next, it's nothing but crickets. And when the gigs dry up, so does your income. Unlike salaried workers who get paid no matter how the business performs, freelancers only eat what they kill. This constant financial uncertainty is why many freelancers burn out before they even break even. Managing this rollercoaster isn't just about working harder—it's about working smarter and building systems that protect your peace *and* your pockets.

One of the biggest traps new freelancers fall into is underselling themselves. When you're starting out, it's tempting to accept any offer that comes your way. You tell yourself, *"I'll raise my rates later,"* but later never comes. Before you know it, you're drowning in low-paying gigs, exhausted, and wondering why you ever left your stable job. Pricing isn't just about what you think you're worth—it's about what your work actually costs to deliver. And if you're not charging enough to cover your time, expenses, and future growth, you're already losing.

Here's the truth: clients will pay what you ask—if you know how to ask for it confidently. The difference between a $500 gig and a $5,000 gig is often just positioning. When you frame your work as a valuable solution rather than a basic service, you shift the power dynamic. You're not just selling hours—you're selling outcomes. And outcomes are always worth more. Successful freelancers treat their pricing like a business decision, not a personal one. They understand that every underpriced project isn't just a financial loss—it's time stolen from future, higher-paying opportunities.

But pricing isn't the only challenge—negotiation is its own battlefield. When you're a freelancer, every client relationship is a negotiation, whether you realize it or not. From defining your scope of work to setting payment terms, the ability to negotiate effectively is the difference between thriving and barely surviving.

Without clear boundaries, clients will push for more—more revisions, more hours, more access. And if you're not careful, you'll give it to them, slowly eroding your profits and sanity.

Smart freelancers know that negotiation isn't about being combative—it's about being clear and firm. It means stating your rates without apology and enforcing policies that protect your time. You're not doing clients a favour—they're paying for your expertise. And if a client doesn't respect your value, that's not your client. Let them go. Because every time you undercharge or overdeliver without compensation, you're reinforcing the idea that your work—and by extension, your time—is cheap.

Even when the work is flowing, another reality hits: managing cash flow. Unlike a 9-to-5 job where money lands in your account like clockwork, freelance income can be unpredictable. Clients pay late. Projects get delayed. And those big, exciting invoices? They're often stretched across 30, 60, even 90 days. In the meantime, your bills don't stop. This is where most freelancers slip up—they treat every payday like a windfall instead of building systems to smooth out the gaps.

Managing cash flow as a freelancer means thinking like a CFO. You can't just spend what you make—you have to plan ahead. Smart freelancers maintain an emergency fund specifically for slow months and always account for taxes. Because yes, when you're self-employed, no one is withholding taxes for you. If you're not careful, tax season will slap you with a bill bigger than any client check. The freelancers who survive long-term are the ones who run their money—not the other way around.

And let's talk about the hidden costs. Freelancing isn't free. Every hour you spend working for a client is time you're not marketing, learning, or growing your business. You're responsible for your own equipment, software, health insurance, and retirement savings. That "freedom" everyone craves? It comes at a price—one you have to be prepared to pay. And unlike a traditional job, there's no paid sick leave, no vacation days, and definitely no company-sponsored wellness retreats. If you're not working, you're not earning. And that can be a terrifying reality.

Still, for all its challenges, freelancing isn't just about survival—it's about sovereignty. Yes, the path is harder, but the rewards are real. You get to choose your clients. You set your hours. You decide how much you earn. And if you're strategic, freelancing becomes more than a hustle—it becomes a vehicle for financial freedom. The key is treating it like a business, not a side project. That means pricing confidently, negotiating smartly, and managing your cash flow like your livelihood depends on it—because it does.

If you're thinking about freelancing, understand this: it's not easy, and it's not always fun. But for those willing to navigate the chaos, it's one of the few career paths where you own your time and your income. In a world where job security is a myth, freelancing isn't just a career choice—it's a survival strategy. And if you do it right, it's the ultimate flex.

9

Passive Income Is a Fantasy—Until You Build It Right

PASSIVE INCOME SOUNDS LIKE THE holy grail of modern work culture—money rolling in while you sleep, travel, or binge-watch your favorite shows. Social media feeds are flooded with influencers promising "easy money" and "automated cash machines," making it seem like anyone with a Wi-Fi connection can get rich overnight. But here's the truth: if it were that easy, everyone would be doing it. Most people chasing passive income end up burned out, frustrated, and disillusioned because they're sold the fantasy but not the framework.

Let's cut through the noise—real passive income is possible, but it's not a quick fix. It takes time, strategy, and yes—work. The key difference between those who succeed and those who get scammed is understanding that passive income isn't about doing nothing—it's about doing the right things *once* and letting those things pay off repeatedly. When done right, it frees you from the endless cycle of trading time for money. But if you go into it expecting instant wealth, you're setting yourself up for disappointment.

Here's the harsh reality: most so-called passive income opportunities are nothing more than thinly-veiled scams. From "drop-shipping empires" to pyramid-shaped affiliate programs, these schemes prey on people who want quick wins without putting in the effort. The problem? Real passive income is rarely quick, and it's never effortless. If someone is promising you a six-figure income with zero skills or work, you're the product—not the beneficiary.

What does work is building assets—things that generate value independently of your time. Think of passive income like a vending machine. You invest upfront by buying the machine and stocking it with products. Once it's in place, you don't need to stand there all day—it earns money while you focus on other things. But getting that machine running? That's where the work happens. Digital products, real estate, intellectual property, and automated services are just a few examples of assets that can pay off repeatedly without constant involvement.

The difference between falling for a scam and building real passive income comes down to this: are you creating value that people genuinely want? If the answer is yes—and you can deliver that value without constant oversight—you're on the right path. But if the model relies on recruiting others or reselling someone else's outdated blueprint, you're likely running in circles.

How to Create Assets That Pay You Long-Term

If you want to escape the active-income grind, start by thinking in assets. What can you build once that people will pay for repeatedly? The good news is, you probably already have skills, knowledge, or expertise that can be turned into an income-generating asset. The challenge is figuring out how to package it effectively.

1. Digital Products – If you know how to solve a problem or teach a skill, turn that knowledge into something people

can buy. E-books, courses, templates, and guides are all examples of digital products that require upfront work but generate long-term revenue. The beauty? Once you create it, you can sell it infinitely without needing to recreate it.

2. Licensing and Intellectual Property – Own something valuable? License it. From artwork and photography to software and patents, licensing lets you earn without actively working. Creators who license their work to companies—whether it's music tracks, designs, or unique processes—make money every time it's used.

3. Affiliate Marketing – Done right, affiliate marketing can be a reliable income stream. Instead of creating products yourself, you earn commissions by recommending other people's products. The trick? Only promote things you genuinely believe in, and focus on building trust with your audience. Sleazy, mass-promotion tactics rarely pay off.

4. Membership and Subscription Models – If you deliver ongoing value, people will pay for continuous access. Membership communities, exclusive content subscriptions, and even specialized newsletters are scalable models that bring in recurring revenue. The key here is consistency—people will pay for sustained value, not one-off hype.

5. Automated Services – You don't need to be present to deliver every service. Automate processes that people will pay for repeatedly. This could be anything from a self-service consulting tool to a database that provides reports or specialized data. Once it's built, it works while you don't.

The foundation of long-term passive income is simple: create things that people want, automate the delivery, and maintain the system to keep the value flowing.

One of the biggest misconceptions about passive income is that it's completely hands-off. In reality, passive income is more like a "front-loaded hustle." You work hard in the beginning to create and refine your system, but once it's operational, the revenue comes without constant effort.

Active hustle—your regular job or freelance work—pays you for your time. You clock in, perform a task, and get paid. When you stop working, the money stops. Passive income, on the other hand, pays you for systems, intellectual property, or products that work on their own. The difference isn't the absence of work—it's the ability to separate your earnings from your daily time investment.

Passive income isn't an excuse to stop working—it's a strategy to work smarter. By building income streams that don't require you to be present 24/7, you unlock time freedom. And in a world where burnout is real and job security is a myth, having income that doesn't rely on your immediate labor is a power move.

Smart Ways to Monetize Your Skills While You Sleep

Think about the skills you already have—chances are, there's a way to monetize them passively. The trick is to focus on scalable, repeatable formats that don't require constant supervision. Some smart ways to do this include:

- Courses & Workshops – Package your expertise into an online course. Use platforms that handle the delivery while you collect payments. Once it's built, it sells itself.
- Digital Downloads – From design templates to business checklists, anything that saves people time is valuable. Create once, sell forever.

- Membership Communities – Curate exclusive content or communities where people pay monthly to access your insights.
- Niche Websites – Build a content-rich website on a specific topic and monetize it through ads, sponsorships, or affiliate links.

The best passive income strategies align with what you're already good at. You don't need to reinvent yourself—you need to amplify your skills in scalable ways.

Here's the truth no one likes to admit: passive income requires *work*. Not forever—but in the beginning. You'll invest time building products, setting up systems, and optimizing processes. But once the groundwork is done, you shift from active effort to automated rewards.

And the payoff? It's freedom. The ability to step away from constant hustle and still make money is the ultimate career flex. Passive income isn't about doing nothing—it's about doing the right things once and letting those things pay you indefinitely. The goal isn't to escape work—it's to escape the trap of working for every dollar.

When you build passive income the right way, you stop trading hours for money. You own your time, your energy, and your future. And that's not a fantasy—it's a power move.

10

From Paycheck to Portfolio— Think Like a Business

A PAYCHECK IS JUST THE beginning—but the real power lies in what you do with it. In a world where traditional job security is fading fast, treating your career like a business and your income like a portfolio isn't just smart—it's survival. The days of relying on a single employer for a lifetime of stability are long gone. Today's most successful people aren't just clocking in and cashing out—they're building diversified revenue streams that work for them. It's not about trading time for money forever; it's about transforming your hard-earned paycheck into a foundation for lasting wealth.

Thinking like a business means approaching your career with intention and strategy. Every skill you develop, every connection you make, and every dollar you earn is part of a larger system that can work in your favor—if you know how to leverage it. This shift starts with recognizing that your job is a tool, not the entire toolbox. Your paycheck is fuel, but what you do with it determines whether you stay on the hamster wheel or build a machine that runs itself. That means stepping away from the mindset of just earning and spending and moving toward a model where your income starts working for you.

At its core, a business thrives on multiple revenue streams—and so should you. Relying on a single paycheck leaves you vulnerable. One layoff, one bad boss, or one industry collapse, and your entire financial foundation can crumble. But when you diversify your income, you create a safety net that protects you from economic shifts and career disruptions. This isn't about working yourself to exhaustion or having five different jobs. It's about strategically building systems that generate revenue in ways that fit your skills, time, and long-term vision.

Start by identifying the areas where your expertise can be monetized beyond your day job. The skills you use daily—writing, design, coding, consulting, teaching—are valuable beyond the confines of your office. And the beauty of the digital age is that you no longer need corporate gatekeepers to monetize your knowledge. Whether through freelancing, creating digital products, or offering services, there are countless ways to leverage what you already know into additional income streams.

The key to building sustainable multiple revenue streams without burnout lies in smart systems, not just more hustle. You don't need to sacrifice your health or sanity chasing more cash. The goal is to create income pathways that eventually require less of your direct involvement. That could mean turning your expertise into a digital course, licensing your intellectual property, or building a membership model where your work delivers value on autopilot. The upfront effort is real—but the long-term payoff is freedom.

Transitioning from employee to entrepreneur doesn't mean quitting your job tomorrow. In fact, the smartest moves often happen when you're still drawing a steady paycheck. That financial foundation allows you to experiment, invest, and grow your side ventures without the immediate pressure to turn a profit. It's about building a bridge—not burning one. Use your current position to fund your future moves. Every extra dollar you earn outside your main job gives you leverage—leverage to negotiate better opportunities, to take career risks, and to eventually walk away from anything that no longer serves you.

Building wealth this way isn't just about making money—it's about making intentional moves that compound over time. Short-term wins are fine, but the real game is in the long play. That means choosing projects and investments that align with your long-term goals. Don't just chase quick cash—build assets that appreciate in value. Whether it's building a brand, investing in real estate, or creating intellectual property, the goal is to construct a portfolio that pays you back long after the initial work is done.

It's also about protecting what you build. Just as a business safeguards its assets, you should be safeguarding your financial future. That means setting up legal protections, reinvesting in your growth, and diversifying your revenue streams so that no single income source can make or break you. The modern economy is unpredictable—but the more control you have over your income sources, the less vulnerable you are to external shifts.

The mindset shift from "worker" to "owner" is where everything changes. Employees trade hours for dollars. Owners create systems that generate wealth whether they're working or not. It's the difference between being stuck on a paycheck treadmill and building a financial machine that moves with or without you. And that shift starts now—by treating every opportunity as a piece of a larger financial puzzle, one that's designed to give you freedom, flexibility, and long-term security.

You don't need to go all-in overnight, but you do need to start playing the game differently. View your career as a business and your paycheck as capital. Invest in yourself, build systems, and prioritize revenue streams that can eventually work without constant input. Because the goal isn't just to earn a living—it's to design a life where your work today funds your freedom tomorrow.

PART 3

Networking Is the New Job Security—Use It or Lose It

11

Your Network Is Your Safety Net—Build It Now

IN A WORLD WHERE JOB security is more myth than reality, your greatest professional asset isn't your résumé—it's your network. Forget the outdated advice about working hard in silence and waiting to be noticed. In today's chaotic job market, it's not just what you know that opens doors—it's who's willing to open them for you. Connections create opportunities. And in an era where layoffs are constant and industries are being reshaped by AI, your network is the ultimate safety net.

But let's be clear—networking isn't about schmoozing at dull corporate events or sending desperate LinkedIn messages when you're out of work. It's about building real, human relationships long before you need them. The people you surround yourself with can be the difference between scrambling for a job after a layoff or getting a heads-up about new roles before they even go public. A strong network isn't a backup plan—it's an ongoing investment in your career's future. And if you're not actively building it now, you're playing a risky game of professional roulette.

The old "meritocracy" myth—that talent alone will carry you to the top—is comforting but incomplete. Of course, skills matter. But the reality is that people hire people they trust. And that trust is built through connections. This doesn't mean you need to fake friendships or become a networking robot. It means recognizing that your relationships are currency in the modern job market—and the sooner you start cultivating them, the richer your career options become.

So, how do you build a powerful network without being that cringey person handing out business cards like candy? It starts with showing up—authentically and consistently. Don't wait until you're in crisis mode to reach out. People can smell desperation a mile away. Instead, invest in your network when you're secure, so when you need support, it's already there. Engage with people in your industry. Attend the virtual panels, the webinars, the conferences. Not because you're hunting for your next job today, but because these spaces are where opportunities quietly circulate.

And here's a truth most people overlook—meaningful connections are built in the small moments, not grand gestures. It's the casual check-in, the "saw this article and thought of you" message, or the LinkedIn comment that keeps you on someone's radar. If you only reach out when you need something, you're not networking—you're extracting. Real relationships are reciprocal. You have to give before you get. Share insights. Celebrate others' wins. Offer help without strings attached. These small acts of generosity compound over time, turning acquaintances into allies.

One of the most underrated secrets of networking? The power of weak ties. It's not always your closest friends or colleagues who unlock life-changing opportunities—it's the people on the periphery of your social circle. A former classmate. That person you met once at a conference. Someone you interact with casually online. Research backs this up—people outside your immediate circle often introduce you to job opportunities you'd never find otherwise. Why? Because they occupy spaces you don't. And when you stay visible and valuable within your extended network, those weak ties become powerful bridges to new possibilities.

Nurturing your network doesn't mean spending hours crafting awkward emails or forcing small talk. It means being intentional about staying connected in ways that feel organic to you. If you hate networking events, skip them—but stay active in digital spaces. Comment thoughtfully on industry conversations. Share your insights. Be curious about what others are working on. And don't underestimate the power of a simple follow-up. A quick "Hey, how's that project going?" is often the difference between being forgotten and staying top of mind.

And when the time comes to tap into your network—whether you're job-hunting, launching a side hustle, or seeking mentorship—do it with clarity and respect. Be specific about what you're asking for. A vague "I'm looking for opportunities" is easy to ignore. But "I'm exploring product management roles in fintech—do you know anyone I should talk to?" is actionable. People want to help, but they can't read your mind. Make it easy for them to connect the dots.

At the same time, don't burn your social capital by over-asking or ghosting once you get what you need. Networking is a long game. The people who sustain successful careers know how to maintain relationships even when they don't immediately "need" anything. That means checking in periodically, sharing useful resources, and showing genuine interest in others' success. Be the kind of person people are happy to hear from—not just when you're in a career pinch, but anytime.

In the end, your network is more than just a professional safety net—it's an ecosystem that grows as you do. It's where new ideas, unexpected collaborations, and future job offers come from. And the stronger that ecosystem, the more resilient your career becomes. Don't wait for a layoff, an industry shake-up, or a career crisis to realize how much your network matters. Build it now. Invest in it consistently. Because in a world where no job is truly secure, the relationships you cultivate today are the opportunities that will carry you forward tomorrow.

12

The LinkedIn Power Move You're Not Making

IF YOU'RE STILL TREATING LINKEDIN like a digital résumé graveyard, you're leaving opportunities on the table. Gone are the days when your profile was just a static list of past jobs and vague skills. Today, LinkedIn is your career billboard—an active, evolving space where recruiters, clients, and industry leaders are watching (yes, even when you think they aren't). And while most people stick to the basics—name, title, a half-baked summary—you have the power to turn your LinkedIn into a magnet for professional opportunities without doing the exhausting "look at me" hustle.

Think of it like this: Every time someone searches your name or a skill you offer, your LinkedIn profile is your first impression. And in a world where first impressions are digital, your profile needs to do more than just list where you've worked—it needs to tell a story that sells your value. The best part? You don't need to be a content creator or a networking savant to pull this off. With a few strategic moves, your LinkedIn can quietly work overtime—opening doors while you focus on the rest of your career.

Start with your headline—because "Marketing Manager" isn't cutting it. Your LinkedIn headline is prime real estate, and yet most people treat it like a boring job label. Instead, think of it as your hook—a one-liner that communicates what you do and why it matters. Compare "Marketing Manager at XYZ Corp" with "I help brands turn followers into loyal customers through data-driven storytelling." One is forgettable. The other tells people exactly what you bring to the table. This subtle shift turns your headline into a pitch, and suddenly, you're no longer just another professional—you're a solution.

Next, there's your bio (or "About" section, if you want to get technical). Most people treat this section like a dry autobiography. Big mistake. Your bio isn't just a place to list achievements—it's your chance to frame your career narrative in a way that resonates with the people you want to attract. A compelling bio does three things: it tells people who you are, highlights what you've accomplished, and—most importantly—shows where you're headed next. Don't just say, "Experienced project manager with 10 years in the industry." Instead, position yourself like a brand: "I specialize in transforming chaotic workflows into efficient systems. With a decade of leading cross-functional teams, I thrive at the intersection of strategy and execution—driving projects from concept to completion on time and on budget." You're not just listing facts—you're showcasing your unique value.

But here's where most people stop. They fill out their profile and assume the work is done. Wrong. The real power move lies in content—because LinkedIn isn't just a place to be found, it's a platform to be heard. Sharing your insights through posts, articles, and comments elevates you from a passive profile to an industry insider. This doesn't mean you need to turn into a full-time thought leader. You can start small—share a quick takeaway from a project, post a question that sparks conversation, or comment meaningfully on others' posts. Every time you engage, you remind your network (and beyond) who you are and what you bring to the table.

And here's a secret: LinkedIn's algorithm loves engagement. The more active you are, the more visible you become. When you share useful insights and interact with others' content, you're not just building your personal brand—you're making it easier for opportunities to find you. And don't underestimate the power of niche conversations. While everyone else is chasing viral posts, the real magic happens in focused discussions where the right people are paying attention. If you're in tech, talk about emerging trends. If you're in finance, break down complex ideas in simple terms. It's not about being everywhere—it's about being where the right people are looking.

Beyond content, LinkedIn hides a few golden features that most people ignore. For example, the "Featured" section lets you pin your best work to the top of your profile—whether that's an article, a project portfolio, or even a media interview. This is where you showcase proof of what you do best. And the "Open to Work" feature? It's more powerful than you think—especially if you customize it for specific roles. LinkedIn quietly notifies recruiters who are searching for candidates like you without blasting it to your entire network.

And let's talk about LinkedIn's search game—because if you're not optimizing your profile for searchability, you're invisible. Every section of your profile is a keyword opportunity. If you want to be found for "product management," those words need to show up in your headline, bio, and skills section. This isn't just about stuffing buzzwords—it's about aligning your profile with the language hiring managers and recruiters actually use. Think of LinkedIn's search bar as a window into how companies find talent. By understanding and integrating relevant keywords naturally, you increase your chances of popping up when someone's looking for your expertise.

Here's another overlooked move—personalizing connection requests. We've all gotten those generic "I'd like to add you to my network" messages, and guess what? They're forgettable. If you're reaching out, take two minutes to craft a personalized note that explains why you want to connect. Something as simple as "I loved your recent post on AI in marketing—would love to stay connected and learn from your insights" makes a world of difference. It shows you're intentional, not just collecting digital trophies.

But there's one thing that matters more than having thousands of connections—actual engagement. Quality beats quantity every time. A tight-knit, engaged network is infinitely more valuable than a bloated one filled with strangers. Curate your network with intention. Follow industry leaders. Connect with peers. And don't just collect contacts—build relationships. This means showing up, contributing to conversations, and offering value without immediately asking for something in return.

If you play it right, LinkedIn stops being a static career archive and becomes a dynamic platform that works for you 24/7. It's your opportunity engine—a space where people with the power to change your career trajectory can find and engage with you. The goal isn't to be everywhere all the time—it's to be in the right places, saying the right things, and making it easy for the right people to see your value. And once you master this, your career stops depending on luck or perfect timing—because you've built a system where opportunities come to you.

13

Clout Won't Pay the Bills— But Credibility Will

IN A WORLD OBSESSED WITH likes, followers, and viral moments, it's easy to fall into the trap of chasing online clout. But here's the uncomfortable truth—clout won't pay your bills. What actually pays? Credibility. Real authority in your industry is the currency that opens doors, lands high-paying opportunities, and gives you staying power long after the latest trend fades.

The problem with clout is that it's fleeting. Today's viral sensation is tomorrow's forgotten name. Online popularity might inflate your ego, but it rarely translates into lasting career success unless you're pairing it with something deeper—expertise. Credibility, on the other hand, is a long game. It's built on substance, not spectacle. And while anyone can rack up likes with a clever meme or a hot take, earning genuine trust takes intention, consistency, and a commitment to delivering real value.

So, what does building credibility actually look like? It starts with knowing your stuff—and showing it. You don't have to be the loudest person in the room, but you do need to make it clear that you know what you're talking about. This means moving beyond surface-level content and offering insights that can't be Googled in five seconds. Anyone can regurgitate industry buzzwords. The people who stand out are the ones who provide fresh perspectives, original ideas, and practical solutions to real problems.

One of the fastest ways to build credibility is by becoming a go-to resource in your niche. Think of yourself as the person others turn to when they need answers. Share case studies from your work. Break down complex topics into digestible insights. Offer frameworks and processes people can actually use. The more you demonstrate your expertise, the more people will associate your name with authority—and the more likely they are to trust you when opportunities arise.

But here's the key: you need to do this consistently. Credibility isn't built on a one-off LinkedIn post or a viral thread. It's the result of showing up repeatedly with value-driven content. And before you panic—no, this doesn't mean you need to churn out daily thought pieces. It means being intentional about how and where you share your expertise. Whether it's contributing to industry publications, speaking at conferences, or simply posting thoughtful insights on social media, your goal is to leave a trail of proof that you know your stuff.

And while we're on the topic—let's get one thing straight. Thought leadership isn't about being famous; it's about being respected. It's easy to get caught up in vanity metrics—likes, retweets, and follower counts—but those numbers are only valuable if they translate into real-world credibility. The best thought leaders aren't chasing clout; they're providing insights that shape conversations and push industries forward. They don't follow trends—they set them.

If you want to play the long game, focus on depth over noise. Anyone can jump on the latest buzzword, but people with true authority dig deeper. Instead of chasing every trend, ask yourself: What are the underlying shifts in my industry? What are the problems no one else is solving? What do I know that others don't? These are the questions that lead to credible, meaningful content that people actually trust.

Of course, showcasing expertise doesn't mean oversharing every detail of your life or work. There's a fine line between offering value and giving away the whole shop. The goal is to demonstrate competence without depleting your intellectual property. Share insights that highlight your approach while leaving room for people to hire you for the full solution. You're not just building a reputation—you're building demand.

And that's the real power of credibility. When people see you as an expert, they come to you—not the other way around. It's the difference between chasing clients and attracting them, between begging for opportunities and being the obvious choice. Employers and clients want to work with people they trust to deliver—and credibility is what makes you that person.

There's also a strategic advantage to credibility that clout can never touch—it compounds over time. When you consistently deliver value, you build a body of work that speaks for itself. And while viral moments fade, your expertise only grows stronger. This means that every panel you speak on, every article you publish, and every thoughtful insight you share adds another layer to your authority. Long after the noise dies down, your reputation continues to work for you.

And don't underestimate the power of association. Credibility isn't just about what you say—it's also about who vouches for you. Being endorsed by other credible people amplifies your authority. This could mean collaborating with industry leaders, contributing to respected platforms, or simply having others reference your work. When people with established credibility co-sign your expertise, it reinforces your position as someone who knows their stuff.

But the real magic happens when you turn that credibility into tangible career opportunities. Once people trust you, they're more likely to hire you, promote you, or bring you into rooms you wouldn't have accessed otherwise. And while clout might get you a few surface-level gigs, credibility is what sustains a career. It's what allows you to raise your rates, pivot industries, or build a personal brand that stands the test of time.

So, where do you start? Focus on building a body of work that reflects your expertise. Share insights that solve real problems. Position yourself as a person of value—not just volume. And most importantly, play the long game. Because while clout is a temporary high, credibility is the foundation for a career that pays—and lasts.

14

Mentors Matter—Find One (Or More)

MENTORSHIP ISN'T A BUZZWORD—IT'S A career cheat code. In a world where job descriptions change overnight, having someone who's been through the trenches can be the difference between struggling in the dark and leveling up faster than your peers. But here's the thing: the old-school idea of one perfect mentor guiding you through your entire career? Dead. The truth is, you need multiple mentors—different people for different seasons of your professional life. Whether you're just starting out, making a pivot, or chasing executive-level goals, having the right people in your corner isn't optional—it's essential.

So, why do mentors matter so much? Simple: they give you what Google can't. Experience. Nuance. The unfiltered truth about how things really work behind the scenes. While everyone else is playing guessing games, a good mentor hands you the map—and sometimes, the keys to rooms you didn't even know existed. And in today's chaotic career landscape, having access to that kind of insight isn't a luxury; it's a necessity.

But let's get one thing straight—mentorship isn't a handout. It's a relationship. The best mentors don't just show up out of nowhere and offer to guide you. You have to seek them out, show your value, and nurture the connection. And no, sliding into someone's DMs with "Will you be my mentor?" isn't the move. Approaching potential mentors requires both intention and finesse. The key? Start by showing genuine interest in their work. Engage with their ideas, ask thoughtful questions, and demonstrate that you're invested in learning—not just in using them as a shortcut.

The biggest mistake people make when searching for mentors is thinking they need one all-powerful guru. You don't need a career soulmate—you need a team. Different people bring different strengths, and the smartest professionals know how to build a mentor portfolio. Think of it like this: you want a mix of mentors who can offer strategic advice, industry-specific knowledge, and real-world wisdom. Some will help you navigate office politics. Others will push your creative boundaries. And some will give you the tough love you didn't know you needed.

And while we're on the topic—let's break down the difference between a coach, a sponsor, and a mentor. A mentor is someone who shares their experiences to help you grow. They give you guidance, perspective, and sometimes a well-timed reality check. A coach, on the other hand, is focused on performance. They're the ones helping you sharpen your skills, hit goals, and improve in specific areas. Sponsors? They're the power players who advocate for you behind closed doors. While mentors talk to you, sponsors talk about you—to the people who can actually change your career trajectory. If you're serious about leveling up, you need all three.

Finding the right mentors requires more than just luck—it's about being proactive. Start by identifying people who are doing what you want to do, but a few steps ahead. These don't need to be CEO-level icons; sometimes, the best mentors are mid-career professionals who still remember what it's like to be where you are. Pay attention to who's thriving in areas you care about. Who's navigating industry changes smoothly? Who's building the kind of career you admire? These are the people worth learning from.

Once you identify potential mentors, focus on building relationships—not extracting value. People are more willing to invest in those who show curiosity, consistency, and a genuine willingness to learn. Don't come in asking for vague "advice." Instead, ask specific questions about their experiences. What decisions shaped their path? What mistakes did they make? What do they wish they'd known earlier? These are the kinds of conversations that foster real connection.

And here's a power move—be useful. The best mentorships aren't one-sided; they're mutually beneficial. You might not think you have anything to offer someone further along, but you do. Maybe you understand emerging tech, have insights on new cultural trends, or can share fresh perspectives that they don't get from their peers. This is where reverse mentoring comes into play—when you bring value to the table, you're not just a mentee. You're a collaborator.

Don't underestimate how valuable your unique knowledge is. In a rapidly changing world, even the most seasoned professionals are hungry to stay ahead. If you can offer them insights they wouldn't otherwise have access to—whether it's decoding the latest social media platform or understanding how Gen Z thinks— you become more than just a mentee. You become indispensable.

Another underrated strategy? Look horizontally—not just vertically. Peer mentors, people at similar career stages but with different strengths, can be just as valuable as more senior figures. Sometimes the best insights come from people who are in the trenches with you, facing similar challenges in real time. And as you all grow in your respective careers, those peer relationships often turn into powerful professional alliances.

The reality is, mentorship accelerates everything. It's like having an inside track on how to win the game while everyone else is still figuring out the rules. A well-timed conversation with the right person can save you years of trial and error. It can mean the difference between being stuck and being unstoppable. But you have to put yourself in the rooms where those conversations happen. Attend industry events, engage in online communities, and never underestimate the value of a casual coffee chat—those moments often lead to career-changing connections.

And when you do secure mentorship, treat it with care. Respect their time, follow through on their advice, and always express gratitude. Mentorship isn't transactional—it's a long-term relationship. When people invest in you, they're not just giving you information—they're giving you access, credibility, and belief in your potential. Honor that by showing up, doing the work, and paying it forward when it's your turn.

Because here's the truth—no one succeeds alone. Behind every thriving career is a network of people who opened doors, shared wisdom, and pushed for their success. If you're serious about building a career that lasts, find your people. And when you do? Hold on tight—because that's when the real magic happens.

15

The Right Connections Make the Hardest Pivots Easy

CAREER PIVOTS AREN'T JUST ABOUT skills—they're about people. In a world where industries evolve faster than job descriptions can keep up, the right connections can turn an intimidating career shift into a strategic power move. Whether you're switching industries, moving into a new role, or building something entirely on your own, one truth remains: who you know is often the bridge between where you are and where you want to be.

The myth of the solo career climb is exactly that—a myth. People love the romantic idea of the self-made professional, hustling alone in the dark until they "make it." But if you peel back the layers of anyone who's made bold, successful career moves, you'll find a network working quietly behind the scenes. It's the former manager who puts in a good word, the industry contact who shares an unlisted opening, the friend who connects you with someone who's already walked the path you're about to take. The reality? No one pivots alone—and the people who try usually struggle longer than they need to.

When you're shifting careers, your existing skills get you part of the way—but it's your relationships that fast-track the process. A warm introduction can open doors no résumé ever will. And while the idea of "networking" often conjures images of awkward mixers and stiff small talk, the best career pivots happen through real, organic relationships—not forced, transactional interactions.

So, how do you network strategically when you're stepping into new territory? It starts with clarity. You can't expect people to help you if you're vague about what you want. Be clear about your pivot—whether that's moving from corporate to creative, jumping industries, or stepping into entrepreneurship. Knowing your direction allows others to guide you effectively. When you reach out for help, be specific: "I'm transitioning into the tech sector, particularly in product management—do you know anyone working in that space I could speak to?" is far more effective than a general, "I'm thinking of switching jobs—any advice?"

Another power move? Start with the people you already know. Most career breakthroughs don't happen through strangers; they come through weak ties—people in your extended network who know of opportunities you aren't aware of. That old college classmate working in your target industry, the former colleague who pivoted successfully—these are your most valuable assets when you're navigating a major career shift. Reach out, reconnect, and let them know what you're working toward. You'd be surprised how often people are willing to help when they know what you're aiming for.

And when you do reach out, lose the awkwardness. Asking for help isn't a sign of weakness—it's a strategic play. The key? Don't make it all about you. Frame your request in a way that's easy for others to say yes to. Instead of a vague "Can you help me find a job?" ask for insight or a small favor. "I know you recently pivoted into marketing—would you be open to a quick call to share how you approached the transition?" is a low-pressure ask. People are more inclined to help when they know you're thoughtful and respectful of their time.

If you're serious about making a pivot, you need to go where the people in your desired field are already gathering. Alumni groups, professional associations, and online communities are gold mines for industry-specific connections. Engage actively—join conversations, share insights, and ask smart questions. These spaces aren't just for lurking—they're opportunities to be seen and remembered by people who can directly impact your next move.

Alumni networks, in particular, are an underutilized resource. People who share your educational background already have a built-in reason to want to see you succeed. Tap into those connections. Universities often host career panels, networking events, and industry-specific forums. Showing up is half the battle—and once you're there, don't be afraid to introduce yourself, share your pivot goals, and follow up with anyone who seems aligned with your path.

The beauty of leveraging your existing circle is that it often leads to the most genuine, long-lasting career relationships. But here's the catch—you have to nurture those relationships long before you need them. The best time to build a professional network is when you're not in crisis mode. If you only reach out when you're job hunting or mid-pivot, it feels transactional. Instead, invest in your network regularly. Celebrate others' successes, share useful resources, and check in without an agenda. That way, when it's your turn to ask for help, the groundwork is already laid.

And don't underestimate the power of reciprocity. Relationships thrive on mutual benefit. When someone helps you, find ways to give back—even if it's just a thank-you note or a thoughtful introduction. Being known as someone who adds value to others' careers makes people far more willing to champion yours. Over time, this approach transforms casual connections into powerful allies who are willing to advocate for you in rooms you may not even know exist.

Your career pivot is only as smooth as the relationships you've built. While others struggle through cold applications and impersonal hiring processes, you can tap into a warm, thriving network that actively pulls you forward. But you have to do the work—reach out, ask smart questions, and offer value in return.

And here's a secret no one tells you: Your next big opportunity is probably already in your circle—you just haven't unlocked it yet. The right connections make even the hardest career pivots easier. So, start today. Build your network with care, invest in people without an agenda, and when it's time to pivot, you won't be doing it alone—you'll have an army behind you, opening doors you couldn't reach on your own.

PART 4

Mastering Career Power Moves—Because Playing Small Won't Work

16

Negotiate Like a Boss—Even When You Feel Powerless

NEGOTIATION ISN'T JUST A SKILL—IT'S a survival tactic in today's volatile job market. Yet, most people treat it like a rare event rather than a regular part of managing their career. Whether you're angling for a raise, a promotion, or better working conditions, negotiation is where real career power lies. And here's the truth: companies always have more wiggle room than they admit. If you don't ask, you leave money—and opportunity—on the table.

The biggest mistake most people make? Believing that the offer they're given is the final word. It's not. Employers expect negotiation; in fact, many have built it into their compensation models. If you accept the first number thrown at you, you're doing their job for them—saving the company money at your own expense. And in a world where corporate budgets stretch for executive bonuses and last-minute hires, trust this: there's always more if you know how to ask.

Timing, however, is everything. Knowing when to negotiate is as crucial as knowing what to say. The best time? When you're at your most valuable—after a major win, at the end of a successful project, or when you've just received a competing offer. If you're starting a new job, the golden window for salary negotiation is *after* you've been offered the role but *before* you sign anything. At this point, they're already invested in you, and the cost of restarting the hiring process makes it easier to give you what you want.

And here's the kicker—negotiation isn't just about the number on your paycheck. Savvy professionals know the real wealth lies in the perks. Remote work options, equity, additional vacation days, professional development funds, or a better job title can be worth more than a modest salary bump. Companies are often more flexible with benefits that don't directly impact their monthly cash flow. If the salary ceiling is firm, pivot to perks that boost your lifestyle and long-term career growth.

But even knowing this, many people freeze when it's time to negotiate. That's where having the right scripts comes in. Forget vague requests like "Is there any flexibility?" and aim for precise, confident language. When negotiating a raise, try: *"Given my contributions over the past year—particularly [X accomplishment]—I believe a salary adjustment to [$ specific amount] is fair. How can we make that happen?"*

If you're negotiating a new offer: *"I'm excited about the opportunity and the impact I can make here. Based on my experience and market standards, I'd be more comfortable with [$ amount]. Is there room to bridge that gap?"*

Notice the framing—you're positioning your request as a logical next step, not an emotional plea. This keeps the conversation professional and puts the onus on them to justify why they *can't* meet your terms. And if you're unsure what to ask for, research is your best weapon. Sites like Glassdoor, Levels.fyi, and LinkedIn Salary can give you real-world salary benchmarks, but don't stop there. Tap your network for inside intel. People in similar roles can provide unfiltered insights that salary websites often miss.

One underrated negotiation tactic? **Silence.** When you make your request, resist the urge to fill the awkward gap. Let the other party speak first. People tend to rush to fill quiet moments—and often, they'll reveal useful information or meet your terms just to break the silence. It's an old-school negotiation trick that still works because most people fear awkward pauses more than losing money.

But negotiation isn't just about the words—it's about mindset. If you walk into the conversation believing you're asking for a favor, you've already lost. You're not begging—you're bringing value, and you deserve to be compensated accordingly. Flip the script in your mind: they're lucky to have *you*. When you understand your worth and approach the conversation from a place of power, you negotiate differently. And it shows.

If your initial request is rejected, don't back down—pivot. Ask, *"What would it take to reach that number in the next six months?"* or *"Are there other ways we can address my request, like additional stock options or performance bonuses?"* This keeps the conversation open and positions you as someone who's both reasonable and persistent—an invaluable combination.

And here's the bold truth: if a company refuses to pay you what you're worth, they probably aren't the right place for you long-term. Staying in a role where you're underpaid and undervalued will drain you faster than any demanding job. There are other companies—and better offers—waiting if you're willing to ask for them.

One of the most powerful negotiation moves? **Having an exit plan.** When you have options—whether it's a side hustle, freelance clients, or other job offers—you negotiate from a position of freedom, not fear. It's harder to push someone around when they know they don't *need* you. The more diverse your income streams, the less power any single employer has over you.

So, next time you're at the negotiation table, remember: You have more leverage than you think. Your work has value. Your time has value. And if you don't advocate for yourself, no one else will. It's not just about getting paid—it's about respecting the work you put in and building a career that reflects your worth. Because playing small doesn't serve you, and in today's economy, it won't keep you safe either.

17

Job Applications Are Rigged— Here's How to Win Anyway

LET'S GET ONE THING STRAIGHT—MOST online job applications are a black hole. You spend hours crafting the perfect résumé, hitting "submit," and then... crickets. No callbacks, no emails, just the void. It's not you—it's the system. Applicant tracking systems (ATS) are designed to filter out more than 75% of résumés before a human even lays eyes on them. If you're relying on the "apply and pray" method, you're already playing a losing game. The modern hiring process isn't about what you know—it's about how you navigate the system. And if you want to win, you have to play smarter.

Here's the harsh truth: most jobs are filled before they're even posted. Companies often promote internally, hire through referrals, or quietly fill roles through professional networks. By the time a job listing hits the internet, you're competing against hundreds—sometimes thousands—of applicants. And guess what? Many of those applicants never stand a chance because the system is rigged to prioritize insider connections and algorithmic matches over actual talent.

So, how do you beat a system designed to shut you out? You find the backdoor—and walk right through it.

Step One: Stop Applying Like Everyone Else

The traditional job application process isn't designed to help you—it's designed to make the company's life easier. The first thing you need to do is break free from the herd. While others are mass-applying to every role in sight, you should be focusing your energy on strategic, high-value moves. That means identifying the companies you want to work for and building relationships *before* a job is ever posted.

Start by making a target list—ten companies you'd love to work for. Follow their key decision-makers on LinkedIn. Engage with their content. If a hiring manager posts about their team's latest project, comment with something insightful. Your goal isn't to be a fan—it's to be on their radar. People hire people they remember.

Step Two: Get in Through the Side Door

Forget waiting for an open job listing—find someone on the inside and make a connection. Internal referrals are the golden ticket to bypassing the ATS maze. According to industry data, candidates referred by current employees are **4x more likely** to get hired. Why? Because companies trust their own people to recommend quality talent.

Here's the move: when you find a job you want, don't just apply—find someone at the company who works in the same department. Send them a concise, professional message like:

"Hey [Name], I admire the work your team is doing at [Company]. I'm particularly interested in [specific project or value they care about]. I noticed a role in [department] and would love to hear your perspective on what makes someone successful there. Would you be open to a quick chat?"

You're not asking for a favor—you're building a bridge. People love to talk about their work, and a well-placed conversation can quickly turn into a referral. If they like you, they'll walk your résumé straight to the hiring manager. No algorithm required.

Step Three: Craft a Pitch That Can't Be Ignored

Your résumé is not a biography—it's a sales pitch. Yet, most applicants treat it like a laundry list of past duties. Stop telling employers what you *did* and start showing them the *impact* you had. Every bullet point on your résumé should answer two questions:

What did you achieve?

Why should anyone care?

Instead of writing: *"Managed social media accounts"*

Try: *"Grew social media engagement by 300% in six months, driving a 25% increase in customer inquiries."*

Results speak louder than responsibilities. Quantify everything—numbers cut through the noise.

And don't stop at the résumé. Your cover letter? It's your secret weapon. Most people treat it as an afterthought, but a well-written cover letter can tip the scales in your favor. Keep it short, sharp, and focused on *how you solve their problems.*

A winning formula looks like this:

1. Open strong—reference something specific about the company that excites you.
2. Connect your skills directly to their needs.
3. Close with a clear call to action: ask for a conversation, not a job.

Example:

"I'm thrilled by [Company's] bold approach to innovation.

My track record of increasing operational efficiency by 40% aligns perfectly with your mission to streamline processes. I'd love to discuss how I can bring this mindset to your team."

Step Four: Follow Up—Because Most People Don't

If you're not following up, you're leaving opportunities on the table. The hiring process is chaotic—emails get lost, decisions stall, and good candidates slip through the cracks. A polite, well-timed follow-up can make all the difference.

If you haven't heard back within a week of applying, send a follow-up email like this:

"Hi [Hiring Manager], I wanted to follow up on my application for [Role]. I'm excited about the opportunity and would love to discuss how my experience in [specific skill or achievement] can contribute to your team. I'm happy to provide any additional information you might need."

This shows you're proactive and genuinely interested. And if you've already had an interview? Always follow up with a thank-you note that reinforces your enthusiasm and reminds them why you're the perfect fit.

Step Five: Play the Long Game

Winning the job game isn't about luck—it's about persistence and strategy. If you don't get the job, don't burn the bridge. Stay connected with the people you met during the process. The job you missed today could turn into an offer tomorrow.

And while you're at it, future-proof your career by building your own brand. Share insights on LinkedIn. Contribute to industry discussions. The more visible you are, the less you'll have to chase jobs—because the best opportunities will find you.

In a world where applications are rigged, being strategic isn't just an advantage—it's survival. So, stop playing by the old rules. Go where the real action happens: behind the scenes, through the right connections, and with a pitch that makes companies sit up and pay attention. The system may be rigged—but you? You're smarter than the system.

18

Rejection Is a Redirection—Use It to Your Advantage

REJECTION STINGS—WHETHER IT'S A "THANKS, but no thanks" email after a job interview or radio silence from a pitch you swore was perfect. It feels personal, even when it's not. But here's the truth no one tells you: rejection is the most valuable career tool you'll ever get—if you know how to use it.

The world moves fast. Jobs change, industries pivot, and even the most qualified people hear "no" more often than "yes." Yet, the people who keep rising aren't the ones who avoid rejection—they're the ones who know how to turn it into leverage. If you're playing the career game, rejection isn't just inevitable—it's a rite of passage. The question is, are you using it to fuel your next big move, or letting it break your momentum?

When you get rejected, it's easy to assume the problem is *you*. Not smart enough. Not experienced enough. Not whatever-enough. But that's not how hiring, promotions, or opportunities really work. Most career decisions are based on factors you'll never see—internal budgets, company politics, or someone else having a relationship with the decision-maker. You're not being rejected because you aren't capable—you're being rejected because, in that moment, someone else fit the puzzle piece they needed.

The people who take rejection personally get stuck in a cycle of self-doubt. But the ones who understand that rejection is situational—not personal—stay in motion. And in a world that rewards persistence, staying in motion is everything.

The Power of Reframing Rejection

Here's a secret that successful people know: rejection isn't a dead end—it's data. Every "no" gives you insider information you didn't have before. Maybe the company wanted a skill set you hadn't highlighted. Maybe they're moving toward a new business model that your background doesn't fit—yet. Either way, rejection is a feedback loop, if you're paying attention.

When you reframe rejection as information—not failure—it becomes a strategic advantage. You start to view every rejection as a step forward, not a step back. Missed out on a job? Now you know what the market wants. Passed over for a promotion? You just learned which skills to sharpen. Each rejection is a clue pointing you toward your next win.

How to Respond to Rejection Like a Pro

The average person hears "no" and ghosts the situation out of embarrassment. The people who win, though? They follow up and stay visible. And that visibility often pays off.

Here's how to respond after a rejection in a way that keeps the door open:

1. Send a Gracious Follow-Up.

A simple, thoughtful message can turn a "no" into a "not yet." Try something like:

"Thank you for considering me for [position]. While I'm disappointed, I'm grateful for the opportunity to connect and

learn more about your team. I'd love to stay in touch and remain interested in future opportunities where my skills could be a fit."

It's professional, leaves the relationship intact, and signals that you're open to future opportunities. Companies remember people who handle rejection well—because most people don't.

2. Ask for Feedback (The Right Way).

Not every rejection comes with an explanation—but asking for feedback is a smart power move. Frame your request in a way that invites honest input without putting anyone on the spot:

"I understand you had many strong candidates. If there's any specific feedback you'd be willing to share, I'd love to use it to improve and grow for future opportunities."

If they respond, you've got actionable intel for your next move. If they don't, you've still signaled that you're serious about growth—a lasting impression.

Rejection Is Fuel—If You Let It Be

Successful people don't just bounce back from rejection—they bounce *forward*. Oprah was told she wasn't fit for television. Steven Spielberg was rejected from film school—three times. Rejection isn't the end of the story; it's the beginning of the rewrite.

So, how do you transform rejection into forward momentum?

Turn "no" into market intel. Every rejection is a free market research report—if you're listening. If you didn't land the job, was it because you're missing a technical skill? If a client didn't choose your service, did they want a different approach? Each "no" reveals gaps you can close. Refine your pitch. Sometimes rejection isn't about your skills—it's about how you're presenting them. If you're hearing no repeatedly, it's time to tweak your story. Are you communicating your value clearly? Are you positioning yourself as the solution to their problem? Each rejection is an opportunity to sharpen your pitch until it becomes undeniable. Build relationships—even after a "no." A rejection doesn't mean the relationship is over. Many people land opportunities months (or even years) after being rejected, simply because they stayed on the radar. Connect with the people who turned you down on LinkedIn. Engage with their content. Stay visible without being pushy. When another opening arises, you'll be top of mind. Play the long game. In today's fast-moving economy, rejection is part of the process. The people who thrive don't let a single "no" derail them—they view rejection as a checkpoint, not a finish line. Keep applying. Keep refining. The more shots you take, the more goals you score.

Here's the thing: most people give up after a "no." They internalize it, shrink back, and stay stuck. But if you use rejection as a tool—not a setback—you gain a serious edge over the competition. While others are licking their wounds, you're collecting insights, building connections, and refining your strategy.

And when you treat rejection as redirection, you stop fearing it altogether. A "no" today is simply a step toward a bigger, better "yes" tomorrow.

So, the next time rejection shows up—and it will—don't let it define you. Let it *inform* you. Let it shape your next move. Because the people who win in this chaotic career landscape aren't the ones who avoid rejection—they're the ones who use it to fuel their greatest success.

19

Career Pivots Are Power Moves—Not Panic Buttons

CAREER PIVOTS ARE OFTEN PAINTED as last-resort moves—desperate leaps taken when everything else falls apart. But that's outdated thinking. In reality, the boldest, most successful careers are built on strategic pivots, not rigid paths. The world is moving too fast for anyone to stay in one lane forever. What was a booming industry five years ago might be on the verge of collapse today. What once felt like your dream job can quickly morph into a dead-end grind. Pivots aren't signs of failure—they're signs of evolution. And the people who embrace that reality are the ones who stay ahead while everyone else clings to fading job security.

The real power of a career pivot isn't just about escaping a job you've outgrown. It's about stepping into the version of yourself you're becoming. The skills, ambitions, and goals that fit you five years ago shouldn't define your next move. As the world changes, you should too. Yet, many people resist the idea of pivoting because it feels like admitting defeat or starting over from scratch. That's a lie. You're never starting from zero—everything you've done so far is part of your leverage. The key is learning how to use your past as fuel, not an anchor.

The fear of a career pivot usually boils down to one question:

"What if I fail?" But the better question is, "What if I stay stuck?" Staying in a role that no longer excites you—or worse, one that's slowly being phased out—comes with a different kind of risk. The longer you cling to comfort, the harder it is to move when you need to. And in a world where industries are being reshaped by AI, automation, and economic shifts, staying still is the most dangerous move of all.

Successful pivots aren't impulsive. They're calculated moves based on recognizing where you are, where the world is going, and how to position yourself at the intersection of both. It's not about abandoning everything you've built—it's about transforming your experience into new opportunities. Think of it like upgrading your operating system. You aren't deleting your skills—you're adapting them to a new environment. And the sooner you realize that everything you've done is transferable, the easier it becomes to make moves that once felt impossible.

One of the biggest misconceptions about pivoting is that you need to know exactly where you're going before you start. That kind of perfectionism keeps people trapped in careers they've outgrown. The truth is, most successful pivots start with a hunch—not a fully mapped-out plan. You don't need to have every detail figured out. You just need to know when your current path is no longer serving you—and have the courage to take the next step.

So, how do you know when it's time to pivot? Pay attention to the friction. When the work that once energized you starts feeling draining, that's not laziness—it's a signal. When opportunities that once excited you start to feel small, that's your ambition outgrowing your current environment. And when you realize your skills could create more impact elsewhere, that's a sign you're ready to move. Most people ignore these signals until they're forced to pivot under pressure. But the smartest career moves happen when you choose to pivot before circumstances make the decision for you.

Making a career pivot doesn't mean burning everything to the ground. It's about stacking your past experiences in ways that open new doors. If you've spent years building a specific expertise, think about how that knowledge can translate across industries. Marketing skills honed in a corporate setting can fuel a shift to tech startups. Project management expertise can pivot into freelance consulting. And communication skills are invaluable everywhere—from leading teams to building your own brand. The key is reframing your narrative. Instead of focusing on job titles, focus on the value you bring. Skills are transferable, and your ability to solve problems is more marketable than any job description.

One of the most overlooked tools in a career pivot is storytelling. The way you frame your career journey can make or break your next move. Employers and clients aren't just looking at your résumé—they're paying attention to how you connect the dots. Instead of apologizing for a non-linear path, own it. A strong pivot story focuses on what you've learned, how those skills apply to new industries, and why your unique perspective makes you an asset. People who master this narrative don't get stuck—they get hired.

And here's the truth most people miss: You don't need permission to pivot. You don't need to wait for your industry to collapse or your boss to push you out. You can start pivoting quietly, on your own terms. That might mean taking on side projects to test new skills. It could look like building relationships in industries you want to break into. Or it might mean investing in learning—whether that's through formal education or self-directed research. The best pivots happen when you move before you have to. By the time everyone else is scrambling, you're already three steps ahead.

There are countless examples of people who pivoted and not only survived—but thrived. Think about it: Oprah started in local news before building a media empire. Jeff Bezos pivoted from Wall Street to launch Amazon. Reese Witherspoon shifted from acting to leading a billion-dollar media company. These aren't stories of people waiting for the "perfect time." They're stories of people recognizing that the world was changing—and positioning themselves to change with it. If you're on the edge of a career pivot, the most powerful thing you can do is trust your instincts. The world is not going to slow down. If anything, change is accelerating. The job you're in today might not even exist a decade from now. And the safest place to be isn't clinging to outdated structures—it's building the skills, relationships, and mindsets that make you adaptable.

Pivoting isn't about panic—it's about power. It's about realizing you are not trapped by your current job, title, or industry. You have the ability to reinvent yourself, over and over again. And in a world that rewards agility, that's the most valuable skill of all. So, if you're waiting for a sign that it's time to make your move—this is it. Pivot while you still have the power. Because the people who pivot by choice are the ones who shape the future, while everyone else is stuck trying to survive it.

20

Quit Like a Strategist—Not an Emotional Wreck

QUITTING A JOB IS RARELY a simple decision. It's easy to fantasize about the dramatic exit—the "take this job and shove it" moment where you finally break free. But real power moves aren't made in anger. They're calculated, strategic, and designed to set you up for the next (better) chapter. Leaving a job isn't just about walking away—it's about walking toward something greater. And the people who quit like strategists, not emotional wrecks, are the ones who land on their feet while everyone else stumbles.

The first step in quitting smart is knowing when it's time to go. Most people wait too long. They hold on, hoping things will improve, while their motivation erodes and their opportunities shrink. Here's the truth: once you've started asking, "Should I quit?"—you're already halfway out the door. Your gut knows before your brain does. But instead of making impulsive decisions, treat your growing dissatisfaction as a signal. If your work no longer challenges you, your values no longer align, or your growth has stalled, it's time to consider an exit. And if you're in a toxic environment that's harming your mental health? You don't need another reason—that's reason enough.

Still, knowing it's time to leave doesn't mean you should

rush the process. Emotional exits often burn bridges and limit future opportunities. The smartest professionals treat quitting like a chess move, not a tantrum. That means getting your next steps in order before you make your announcement. Update your résumé and digital presence. Quietly reach out to your network. Start identifying new opportunities while you're still in your current role—because it's always easier to find your next move while you're employed. And if you're building a side hustle, let it gain momentum before you cut the cord.

Your exit strategy also involves timing. Quitting without a plan feels freeing for about five minutes—until reality hits. The right time to leave is when you're prepared, not when you're overwhelmed. If you've got financial stability, a strong professional network, and a clear vision for your next chapter, you're in a position of power. On the flip side, if you're financially vulnerable or unclear about your next step, take the time to shore up your resources before making the leap. Strategic quitting isn't about escape—it's about setting yourself up for long-term success.

Once you're ready to resign, the way you do it matters. No matter how much you despise your job—or your boss—your exit leaves a lasting impression. And industries are smaller than you think. Today's annoying manager could be tomorrow's key reference. Keep your resignation professional, concise, and free from emotional baggage. Have a clear, simple statement prepared: "I've decided to move on to pursue new opportunities." You don't need to justify your decision, and you definitely don't need to air your grievances. Save those for your group chat.

Delivering your resignation in person (or via video if you're remote) shows respect and professionalism. Avoid the impulse to send a cold email or, worse, ghost your employer. Handing in your resignation face-to-face gives you control over the narrative. It also allows you to express gratitude, which—even if you've had a rough experience—can leave the door open for future collaboration. And never underestimate the power of a thoughtful resignation letter. Keep it brief, positive, and forward-focused. The goal is to make your departure feel like a natural, professional evolution—not a dramatic breakup.

But here's the part most people overlook: your work isn't done once you resign. Your final weeks on the job can either enhance your professional reputation—or destroy it. Treat those weeks as your legacy. Document your processes and ensure a smooth handover. If you manage projects, leave clear instructions for the next person. If you work with clients, introduce them to your replacement. A graceful exit shows you're not just thinking about yourself—you're thinking about the team you're leaving behind. And that kind of professionalism sticks.

It's also the perfect time to strengthen your network. Before you walk out the door, connect with colleagues on LinkedIn, schedule coffee chats with key contacts, and express appreciation to those who supported your growth. Those relationships are your career insurance policy. You never know when a former coworker could become a future collaborator, employer, or referral. Don't disappear without leaving a trail of goodwill behind.

And while you're tying up loose ends, don't forget to future-proof yourself. Download any personal documents you might need, like performance reviews or work samples (without breaching company policy). Clarify your benefits—especially health coverage and unused paid time off. If your job offered professional development resources, use them before you leave. And if you've built valuable skills during your time there, be ready to articulate them in your next role. Your exit should be as strategic as your entrance.

Here's the thing: quitting a job isn't just about leaving—it's about leveling up. Your resignation isn't an ending; it's a pivot point. It's a chance to redefine your career on your terms. So, instead of treating your exit as a reactive decision, use it to accelerate your growth. Think about the lessons you're taking with you. The relationships you're preserving. The doors you're keeping open. When you approach quitting with strategy instead of emotion, you don't just close a chapter—you write the next one on your terms.

And if you're worried about how people will perceive your departure, remember this: your career is not a loyalty contest. You don't owe a lifetime to any job. What you owe yourself is the freedom to evolve. The people who play small—staying in roles they've outgrown out of fear—are the ones who lose momentum. The people who quit strategically? They're the ones who stay in control, no matter how the job market shifts.

So, if you know it's time to walk away, do it with intention. Be calm, be clear, and be calculated. Because quitting isn't weakness—it's power. And when you quit like a strategist, you aren't just leaving a job. You're making your next power move.

PART 5

Future-Proof Your Career—Because Chaos Isn't Slowing Down

21

Think Like a Brand

CAREER ANXIETY ISN'T JUST A passing worry—it's the persistent hum in the back of your mind that asks, "Am I doing enough? Am I falling behind? What if I screw this up?" In an era where job security feels like a myth and the rules of success are constantly shifting, it's no wonder so many people feel like they're one misstep away from chaos. The pressure to "figure it all out" while staying ahead of the curve is exhausting, especially when social media bombards you with everyone else's highlight reel. But here's the truth: career anxiety is not a sign that you're weak or failing—it's a completely normal response to a world where uncertainty is the new normal.

At its core, career anxiety is about control—or the fear of losing it. Humans crave predictability. We want to believe that if we work hard, follow the rules, and check the right boxes, everything will fall into place. But modern careers don't work that way. Industries evolve overnight, algorithms dictate visibility, and layoffs can happen no matter how talented you are. The old promise of a linear career path is gone, and in its place is a reality where you're constantly navigating new terrain. That unpredictability fuels anxiety—especially for people who are used to being in control.

One of the most common triggers of career anxiety is the

fear of the future. Your mind spirals into worst-case scenarios: What if I lose my job? What if I never find my "dream career"? What if I'm falling behind while everyone else speeds ahead? This "future freakout" isn't just mental noise—it's your brain's way of trying to protect you from the unknown. The problem is, anxiety doesn't make you safer—it makes you stuck. When you live in a state of constant worry, you make decisions from a place of fear instead of strategy. And fear-based decisions rarely lead to long-term success.

The first step to handling career anxiety is recognizing that those anxious thoughts are not facts. Your mind might tell you that you're failing—but that doesn't make it true. Instead of getting trapped in a loop of catastrophic thinking, bring yourself back to the present. What can you control today? What's the next best step you can take right now? Breaking big, overwhelming questions into small, actionable steps is a proven way to disrupt anxiety's grip on your mind. You don't need to have your entire career mapped out. You just need to focus on what's directly in front of you.

Another powerful antidote to career anxiety is self-compassion—a concept that high achievers often struggle with the most. When you're ambitious, it's easy to treat yourself like a never-ending project. You celebrate wins briefly but punish yourself relentlessly for mistakes. That internal pressure might feel productive—but over time, it erodes your confidence and resilience. Self-compassion isn't about lowering your standards—it's about giving yourself grace while you pursue ambitious goals. It's recognizing that you are human—not a machine—and you deserve kindness even when you fall short. Research shows that people who practice self-compassion handle setbacks better, bounce back faster, and experience less burnout over time.

Overachievers are particularly vulnerable to career anxiety because they tie their self-worth to their work. When your identity is wrapped up in your professional achievements, any setback feels like a personal failure. If you don't land the promotion, if your project flops, if you get laid off—it doesn't just feel like a professional loss. It feels like you, as a person, are not enough. This is why some of the most outwardly successful people are also the most anxious. They're trapped in a cycle where nothing is ever "enough" to quiet the voice in their head telling them to do more.

The irony? The constant pressure to be perfect actually makes you less effective. Chronic anxiety drains your cognitive resources, making it harder to focus, problem-solve, and think creatively. When you're in a state of fight-or-flight, your brain isn't optimizing for long-term strategy—it's just trying to survive. That's why the most successful people aren't the ones who never feel anxiety—they're the ones who've learned to work with it instead of against it. They know how to pause, recalibrate, and keep moving forward even when their inner critic is screaming.

Science-backed strategies for managing career anxiety focus on calming your nervous system while shifting your perspective. One of the simplest and most effective tools is breathwork. When you're anxious, your body responds as if you're under physical threat—heart racing, muscles tense, mind on overdrive. Deep, intentional breathing activates your parasympathetic nervous system, signaling to your brain that you're safe. Try this: inhale for four counts, hold for four, exhale for six. That extended exhale is the secret—it cues your body to relax.

Another evidence-based strategy is cognitive reframing—challenging the negative stories anxiety tells you. Instead of accepting your anxious thoughts as truth, interrogate them. Is it *really* true that you're falling behind? Is one rejection *actually* proof that you'll never succeed? Probably not. Your brain is wired to focus on threats, but you have the power to redirect that focus. Every time you reframe an anxious thought into a more balanced perspective, you weaken anxiety's grip.

Movement also plays a critical role in managing career anxiety. Exercise isn't just about physical health—it's one of the most powerful ways to regulate your mood. When you're stuck in your head, movement brings you back into your body. Whether it's a ten-minute walk or a full workout, physical activity releases endorphins, reduces stress hormones, and gives your mind a reset. It's not about "working off" anxiety—it's about reminding your nervous system that you're in control.

And here's the truth no one talks about: you don't have to handle career anxiety alone. Too many people suffer in silence, believing they need to "tough it out" on their own. But anxiety loses power when it's shared. Talking to a mentor, therapist, or trusted friend can offer both practical solutions and emotional relief. Sometimes, the simple act of saying, "I'm struggling with this," is enough to loosen anxiety's grip.

At the end of the day, career anxiety is not a sign that you're weak—it's proof that you care. You care about your future. You care about making an impact. You care about living a life that's bigger than a paycheck. That kind of ambition will always come with moments of doubt—but it doesn't have to control you. You have more power than you realize. Not to eliminate anxiety entirely—that's impossible—but to hold it with compassion while you keep moving forward.

Because the truth is, no one has it all figured out. Even the most successful people you admire have felt lost, scared, and unsure at some point. What sets them apart isn't that they never feel anxious—it's that they don't let anxiety stop them. And neither should you. Your career isn't a straight line. It's a series of pivots, risks, and bold moves. And you are far more capable of navigating the uncertainty than your anxiety would have you believe.

22

Soft Skills Are Hard Currency

BURNOUT ISN'T JUST BEING TIRED—IT'S a slow unraveling of everything that makes you feel human. It's the creeping numbness when your passion turns into exhaustion, when even small tasks feel heavy, and when no amount of rest seems to recharge you. And yet, in a culture that glorifies the grind, burnout is often worn like a badge of honor—proof that you're hustling hard enough to deserve success. But here's the truth: burnout isn't a sign that you're committed—it's a flashing red warning light that something is broken. And if you ignore it long enough, it will break you too.

The early signs of burnout are easy to dismiss because they often masquerade as "just being busy." You tell yourself it's normal to feel tired after a long day, to push through a few late nights, to grind a little harder. But burnout doesn't happen overnight—it's a slow accumulation of micro-stressors. The constant pressure to deliver. The feeling that there's never enough time. The anxiety that if you slow down, someone else will take your place. These daily stressors stack up until one day you realize you don't even recognize yourself. Your energy is gone, your creativity is drained, and no matter how much you try to rally, your mind and body say, "Enough."

One of the first red flags of burnout is emotional depletion.

You become irritable over things that wouldn't normally bother you. Small inconveniences feel like personal attacks. You lose the ability to care deeply—about your work, your relationships, even yourself. This emotional exhaustion isn't laziness; it's your brain's way of conserving energy because it's been operating in survival mode for too long. You're not failing—you're overloaded. And without intervention, that emotional depletion can spiral into cynicism, detachment, and a deep sense of disillusionment.

The rise of hustle culture has only made burnout worse. Social media is flooded with the gospel of "grind now, shine later," pushing the idea that rest is a weakness and overwork is a virtue. People brag about 80-hour workweeks like it's a competition—as if running yourself into the ground is the price of success. But here's the uncomfortable reality: hustle culture is a trap. It convinces you that if you're not exhausted, you're not doing enough. And while you're busy proving your worth through work, your health, relationships, and sense of self are quietly deteriorating.

What no one tells you about burnout is how deeply personal the toll is. It's not just physical fatigue—it's emotional erosion. It's the loss of joy in things you once loved. It's waking up already dreading the day ahead. It's the crushing guilt of feeling unproductive even when your body is screaming for rest. And the cruelest part? Burnout doesn't just affect your work—it spills into every corner of your life. You snap at the people you love. You withdraw from friendships because you "don't have the energy." You start to wonder if the life you're chasing is even worth it.

Escaping burnout doesn't mean quitting your ambitions—it means redefining how you pursue them. You can still want big things without sacrificing yourself in the process. And it starts with dismantling the lie that rest is unproductive. Rest isn't a reward you earn after pushing yourself to the brink—it's the foundation that makes sustainable success possible. Without it, you're just sprinting toward a finish line that never arrives.

If you're already deep in burnout, the road back can feel impossible—but it's not. The first step is giving yourself permission to stop pretending you're fine. Acknowledge that burnout isn't a sign of weakness—it's a sign that you've been carrying too much for too long. From there, the work is about recalibrating—not giving up. Identify the areas where you're overextending yourself and start making changes. This might mean setting firmer boundaries with your time, delegating tasks, or re-evaluating commitments that drain you without adding value.

One of the most important shifts is learning to rest without guilt. High achievers often struggle with rest because they equate it with being unproductive. But true rest isn't just "not working"—it's actively restoring yourself. That means making space for activities that replenish your mental, emotional, and physical energy. It's not scrolling mindlessly on your phone while feeling guilty about your to-do list. It's engaging in practices that refill your cup—whether that's spending time in nature, moving your body, connecting with loved ones, or simply allowing yourself to do nothing.

Rebuilding after burnout also requires confronting the beliefs that got you there. What stories are you telling yourself about success? Do you believe you have to suffer to deserve it? Are you afraid that slowing down means falling behind? These narratives are powerful—but they're not the truth. You can be ambitious without being self-destructive. You can want more while still protecting your energy. And you can redefine success on your own terms—one that includes rest, joy, and longevity.

Protecting yourself from future burnout isn't about avoiding hard work—it's about working smarter while safeguarding your well-being. It means treating your energy like a finite resource, not an unlimited one. Pay attention to what drains you versus what energizes you. Practice saying no to opportunities that don't align with your values or capacity. And most importantly, prioritize rest as a non-negotiable—because burnout is far more expensive than taking a break.

Ambition and rest aren't opposites—they're partners. The people who sustain long-term success aren't the ones who burn themselves out—they're the ones who know when to push and when to pause. You don't have to break yourself to prove your worth. In fact, the most powerful thing you can do is refuse to play the game that glorifies burnout. Your ambition is valid—but so is your well-being. And if you want to play the long game, protecting your energy isn't optional—it's essential.

<h1 style="text-align:center">23</h1>

The Hybrid Work Hustle

IMPOSTER SYNDROME ISN'T A PHASE you simply grow out of—it's a shadow that shows up every time you step into something bigger. It doesn't matter how many wins you rack up or how qualified you are; the voice in your head still whispers, *"You don't belong here."* And the irony? The more you achieve, the louder that voice often gets. High achievers—yes, the ones you admire—are the most likely to wrestle with imposter syndrome because they're constantly pushing beyond their comfort zones. When you're always leveling up, there's no "final form" where you suddenly feel invincible. The key isn't to banish imposter syndrome entirely—it's to outsmart it.

At its core, imposter syndrome is a mental glitch where your brain refuses to connect your success to your abilities. Instead of owning your achievements, you chalk them up to luck, timing, or someone else's mistake in giving you a shot. That inner critic tells you that if people really knew how unqualified you are, they'd kick you out. This isn't just a confidence issue—it's a psychological pattern rooted in how you process self-worth and external validation. And the kicker? The more competent you actually are, the more you question yourself because you're aware of how much you *don't* know.

The connection between imposter syndrome and success is

real because self-doubt often walks hand-in-hand with growth. When you're playing small, you rarely feel like a fraud—because you're not stretching yourself. But the moment you start occupying bigger spaces—whether it's a promotion, a new industry, or a public-facing role—that doubt creeps in. It's not a sign you're failing. It's a sign you're expanding. Imposter syndrome isn't proof you're not good enough—it's proof that you're stepping into something that challenges you.

One of the most effective ways to outsmart imposter syndrome is to catch your inner critic in the act. That voice in your head? It's not the objective truth—it's just a voice. And most of the time, it's lying to you. When you hear thoughts like, *"I'm not ready,"* or *"I just got lucky,"* pause and interrogate them. What's the actual evidence? Did you stumble into every opportunity by accident? Or did your work—your ideas, your effort, your expertise—play a part? Your brain will try to discount your success, but you can choose not to buy into the narrative.

The trap most people fall into is waiting for confidence to arrive before they make bold moves. But here's the truth: confidence is a byproduct of action, not the other way around. You don't magically feel ready before you take the leap—you take the leap, and *then* you build confidence by realizing you can handle it. The more you act in the face of imposter syndrome, the less power it holds. Every time you speak up in a meeting, apply for a bigger role, or share your ideas publicly, you're collecting evidence that you're capable. And over time, that evidence starts to outweigh the self-doubt.

Reframing self-doubt as a sign of growth is a game-changer. When that voice pipes up, instead of thinking, *"I must not be good enough,"* flip the script: *"This means I'm stretching into something new.*" The presence of imposter syndrome doesn't mean you're unqualified—it means you're in the arena. And the people who win long-term are the ones who stay in the game despite the doubt. Your inner critic will always have something to say—but it doesn't get the final vote on your worth or your abilities.

Another power move against imposter syndrome? Normalize your feelings by talking about them. The most successful people you admire? They feel it too—they're just better at not letting it stop them. When you open up about imposter syndrome with people you trust, you realize you're not alone. And that shared humanity makes it easier to brush off the belief that you're a fraud. Everyone—no matter how accomplished—has moments where they feel like they're faking it. The difference is whether you let that feeling run the show.

It also helps to shift your focus from perfection to contribution. Imposter syndrome thrives when you obsess over being flawless. But nobody's hiring you, following you, or listening to you because you're perfect—they're doing it because you bring something valuable to the table. Instead of fixating on whether you're *enough*, ask yourself: *"How can I add value here?"* When you focus on serving others—sharing insights, solving problems, making an impact—you redirect your energy toward what matters. And the more you show up and deliver, the quieter that imposter voice becomes.

The sneaky thing about imposter syndrome is that it doesn't disappear with external validation. You could collect every accolade in the book and still feel like you're faking it. That's because imposter syndrome is an *inside job*. It's not about convincing the world you belong—it's about convincing *yourself.* And that takes intentional work. Practice recognizing your wins— big and small. Document them if you have to. When your brain tries to gaslight you into thinking you don't deserve your place, receipts don't lie.

Here's the bottom line: you're never going to wake up one day and feel 100% certain you belong in every room you enter. But you don't need absolute certainty to succeed—you just need to keep showing up. Imposter syndrome only has power if you let it shrink you. When you choose to keep moving forward— speaking up, applying, creating, leading—you take that power back. And eventually, you realize something profound: the voice in your head never had the final say. You did.

24

Play the Game Without Losing Yourself

SUCCESS GUILT IS THE UNSPOKEN weight that creeps in when you start to achieve more than you ever expected—especially when the people around you are still struggling. It's that quiet voice in your head questioning, *"Why me?"* when things are going well, or the discomfort you feel when you realize you're outpacing your peers. Instead of fully celebrating your wins, you downplay them. You shrink in conversations. You feel like you have to apologize for getting ahead while others are still figuring it out. And while no one talks about it openly, success guilt is far more common than you think.

The truth is, society is much more comfortable with struggle than it is with success. We know how to offer empathy when someone is going through a hard time—but when someone's thriving? That's where things get tricky. If you're doing well, you risk being seen as boastful, out of touch, or—worst of all—lucky. So, you learn to dim your light. You soften your wins. You tell yourself not to "make a big deal out of it." And in the process, you hold yourself back from fully stepping into the power your success has earned.

One major driver of success guilt is outpacing your peers.

When you start hitting milestones—whether it's a higher salary, a better job, or a life upgrade—it can feel like you're breaking some unspoken loyalty pact. You worry about leaving people behind or being seen as "too much." And if your circle isn't evolving with you, that guilt can be amplified. It's natural to want to stay connected to the people who shaped you. But here's the truth: real friends want to see you win. If your success makes someone uncomfortable, that says more about their insecurities than your worth.

Another layer of success guilt comes from internalized limits—deep-rooted beliefs about what you think you deserve. If you grew up in environments where money was tight or opportunities were scarce, achieving more can feel…wrong. You might feel like you're betraying your roots or abandoning the version of yourself who struggled. But here's the reality: shrinking yourself doesn't serve anyone. Playing small won't pull others up—it just keeps you stuck. When you break past those internalized limits, you don't just win for yourself—you expand what's possible for everyone watching.

The guilt intensifies in tough economic climates. When layoffs, rising costs, and instability dominate the news, it can feel uncomfortable—even selfish—to enjoy your wins. You might feel like you shouldn't be happy when so many others are struggling. But here's the thing: your success doesn't take away from anyone else's. There's no universal scoreboard where your gain means someone else's loss. In fact, when you own your success, you create more opportunities. You inspire others to stretch beyond their circumstances. Hiding your achievements doesn't ease anyone's burden—but sharing your story can open doors for others.

So, how do you release the guilt and own your success without apology? It starts by recognizing that your achievements are not accidental. You didn't stumble into them by luck—you earned them. The long nights, the risks you took, the resilience you showed—none of that was random. And while external factors like privilege or timing can play a role, they don't negate the work you've put in. You are allowed to own every bit of your success without explaining it away.

It also means separating your self-worth from other people's comfort. You can't control how others perceive your success—but you can control how much you let their opinions shape you. Not everyone will clap when you win, and that's okay. Your life isn't a democracy where everyone else gets a vote. The people who genuinely support you will celebrate you—full stop. And if your success triggers envy or judgment in others, that's their work to unpack—not yours.

Reframing success as a responsibility rather than a burden helps dismantle the guilt. Instead of feeling bad about what you've achieved, ask yourself: *"How can I use my success to uplift others?"* Success isn't just about personal gain—it's about creating ripple effects. Maybe that means mentoring someone who's where you once were. Maybe it means sharing resources, knowledge, or connections. But here's the key: you can only give from a place of abundance. Shrinking yourself doesn't help anyone—but owning your success allows you to be a force for change.

And let's talk about joy—because you're allowed to feel it. You don't need to apologize for loving your life. You're not selfish for being proud of what you've built. Success isn't something you "get away with"—it's something you embody. Denying yourself joy doesn't make the world fairer—it just makes your world smaller. So, give yourself permission to celebrate without guilt. You deserve to experience the fullness of your wins without diminishing them to make others comfortable.

Owning your success also means recognizing that you are still a work in progress—and that's okay. You can be proud of how far you've come while still being ambitious about what's next. Success isn't a final destination—it's an ongoing journey of growth, impact, and evolution. And when you let go of the guilt, you give yourself the freedom to pursue even bigger dreams without hesitation.

At the end of the day, success guilt is just a story your mind tells you—a story you can rewrite. You don't owe anyone an apology for thriving. You don't need to justify your wins. You're not leaving anyone behind by growing—you're paving the way. And the sooner you release the guilt, the sooner you'll step fully into the power and possibility that your success has created. So, take up space. Own your wins. And never, ever apologize for shining.

25

Recession-Proof Careers Start with Smart Choices Now

FAILURE ISN'T THE END OF the road—it's the fuel that drives your next breakthrough. In a world where career paths are no longer linear, failure isn't just inevitable—it's essential. The people who succeed in the long run aren't the ones who avoid failure altogether—they're the ones who know how to extract value from every misstep and keep moving forward. Yet, society has wired us to fear failure like it's a permanent stain on our worth. We glorify success stories but skim over the chapters where things fell apart. What gets lost in this highlight-reel culture is the truth: the biggest wins often come from the lessons failure teaches—if you're bold enough to embrace them.

Modern careers are built on trial and error. Whether you're pivoting to a new industry, launching a side hustle, or negotiating for a promotion, you're going to get things wrong. And that's not a sign you're failing—it's a sign you're playing the game. In fast-moving industries where the rules change constantly, perfection is a myth. You can't wait until you have everything figured out before making a move because by the time you do, the landscape will have shifted again. Failure isn't a sign you're off track—it's proof you're in motion. And motion is the only thing that guarantees progress.

But not all failures are created equal. There's a massive difference between productive and pointless failures. Productive failures are the ones you learn from—the ones that stretch your skills, expose blind spots, and push you to evolve. Pointless failures, on the other hand, are the ones you repeat because you're not paying attention. The difference comes down to reflection. When things go wrong, most people either wallow in self-pity or rush to the next thing without asking, *"What did this teach me?"* But if you can get curious instead of defensive, every failure becomes a masterclass. What worked? What didn't? What would you do differently next time? That's where the gold is—and it's how failure becomes a tool instead of a trap.

The real power move isn't avoiding failure—it's bouncing back faster when it happens. Most people waste too much time sitting in the rubble, replaying mistakes like they're permanent. The truth? You can always rebuild—usually quicker than you think. The key is to move through failure without letting it stick to your identity. You failed—that doesn't mean *you are a failure.* The faster you separate the event from your worth, the faster you regain momentum. It's not about ignoring your feelings—grieve the loss, process the disappointment—but don't unpack and live there. Your career is a long game, and one setback doesn't cancel the whole season.

What's even more powerful? Turning your mistakes into a competitive edge. Most people hide their failures, hoping no one notices—but when you own them, you become untouchable. You show that you can handle pressure, adapt to change, and come back stronger. In fact, the most compelling career narratives aren't the perfect ones—they're the comeback stories. Employers, clients, and collaborators aren't looking for flawless people—they want people who can handle the messy, unpredictable reality of modern work. So instead of covering up your failures, frame them as evidence of your resilience. "I made this mistake, and here's what I did next." That's not weakness—that's leadership.

And let's talk about the elephant in the room—public failure. In the age of social media, it feels like every misstep is on display. The fear of failing in front of an audience can be paralyzing. But here's the truth no one tells you: public failure often leads to private breakthroughs. When you fail in a visible way, you attract the attention of people who know how to help—people who've been there, made the same mistakes, and found their way through. Some of the best opportunities arise after public missteps because the people watching aren't just critics—they're potential allies. But they can't offer help if you're too busy hiding. Being transparent about your failures doesn't just humanize you—it opens doors you never expected.

There's also an unexpected freedom that comes from failing publicly—it strips away the illusion that you need to be perfect. Once you survive a visible flop, you realize it doesn't define you. The fear loses its grip, and you get braver. You stop playing safe. You take bolder risks. Because once you've been knocked down and stood back up, you know you can survive it—and that makes you unstoppable.

The most successful people aren't the ones who never fail—they're the ones who redefine failure entirely. To them, failure isn't fatal—it's feedback. Every misstep is an information download that makes them sharper, smarter, and more strategic. They're not afraid to take chances because they know that even if they fall, they'll rise again—armed with new insights. And that's the mindset shift that changes everything: failure isn't the opposite of success—it's the raw material that builds it.

The next time you stumble, ask yourself: *"What is this teaching me that I couldn't have learned any other way?"* Because there are insights you can only gain through experience—through trying, failing, and recalibrating. No book, podcast, or mentor can teach you the lessons that only your own failures reveal. And when you embrace that truth, failure stops feeling like a threat and starts becoming a tool—a tool you can wield to carve out a career on your terms.

At the end of the day, the only real failure is quitting on yourself. Everything else? It's just a plot twist in your story—a story you're still writing. So, fail boldly. Fail often. And let every failure fuel the future you're building—because the ones who dare to fail are the ones who rise the highest.

PART 6

The New Rules of Career Success—Play to Win

26

Stop Waiting for Promotions

FOR YEARS, WE'VE BEEN SPOON-FED the same corporate bedtime story: if you work hard enough, stay organized, and follow the right routine, you'll unlock the mythical state of *work-life balance.* A harmonious, Pinterest-perfect life where you excel at your job, maintain a buzzing social life, hit the gym five times a week, and somehow still have time to meditate and cook gourmet meals. Spoiler alert—that's not how reality works.

In today's 24/7, always-on world, the very idea of balance feels outdated. Work bleeds into life, life interrupts work, and the old model of a neat, 9-to-5 job with clear boundaries is practically extinct. Emails don't respect office hours, Slack pings don't care if it's family dinner time, and for anyone juggling multiple income streams, the lines between professional and personal can feel permanently blurred. And yet, the conversation still revolves around *balance,* as if finding the perfect ratio of work-to-life is the ultimate achievement.

But here's the truth: balance isn't the goal—control is.

The people who thrive in the modern workforce aren't chasing balance—they're building lives where they call the shots. They don't wait for someone else to hand them more free time or flexibility. Instead, they take ownership of their schedules, energy, and priorities. And that's the shift you need to make if you want to survive—and thrive—in this new world of work.

If you've ever felt like your job is swallowing your life, that's because it probably is. Modern work culture is built on a fundamental truth: work will expand to fill every available space you give it. If you're willing to answer emails at midnight, take last-minute calls on weekends, or let your boss interrupt your vacation, the system will gladly let you. The corporate machine isn't programmed to protect your well-being—it's optimized for output.

The people who master work-life control understand this and act accordingly. They know that if you want to protect your time, you have to be the one drawing the line. That means setting firm boundaries—not just in theory, but in practice. It means deciding what parts of your life are sacred and refusing to let work encroach on them. Because no one else will enforce those boundaries for you.

Define Your Non-Negotiables—And Defend Them

Control starts with clarity. If you don't know what you're protecting, it's easy to let everything blur together. That's why you need to identify your *non-negotiables*—the parts of your life that are off-limits, no matter how demanding work gets. These are the things that keep you grounded, sane, and whole.

Your non-negotiables might look like:

No work after 7 PM—because evenings are for family or personal recharge.

One unplugged day per week—a full 24 hours where no emails, pings, or notifications touch your life.

Physical health first—your workout isn't "extra," it's a critical investment in your energy.

Once you define these, the real work begins: protecting them without apology. It's easy to say you value your time. It's harder to hold that line when a demanding boss, a last-minute request, or career FOMO starts creeping in. But if you don't enforce your boundaries, no one else will.

Boundaries Aren't a Luxury—They're a Career Survival Skill

Let's be clear: setting boundaries isn't a sign of laziness or entitlement. It's a professional power move. When you clearly define and defend your time, you're sending a powerful message: I value my work—but I also value myself. That kind of clarity earns respect.

The fear, of course, is that saying no will make you seem difficult or uncommitted. But the reality? People respect boundaries when you set them with confidence. The trick is to frame your boundaries in ways that prioritize mutual respect and shared outcomes.

Instead of saying:

- "I can't take that call—I'm off."

Try:

- "I'm available until 6 PM—let's schedule something before then."

It's a subtle shift, but it matters. You're not rejecting the work—you're offering a clear framework for how and when you'll engage. This keeps you in control while signaling that you take your commitments seriously.

Saying No Isn't a Career Killer—It's a Career Protector

The biggest myth in modern work culture is that saying yes to everything makes you indispensable. It doesn't. Overcommitting leads to burnout—and burnt-out people aren't making bold career moves. The real power lies in saying no strategically.

The key is to frame your "no" in a way that protects your time while keeping relationships intact. Here are some examples:

When the request isn't urgent:
"I'd love to dive into this—can we circle back next week?"

When you're already at capacity:
"I'm currently at full bandwidth, but I can revisit this next quarter."

When it's outside your scope:
"This falls outside my core focus, but I can connect you with someone who's a great fit."

Each response maintains professionalism while asserting your limits. And over time, people will begin to respect those limits—because you do.

Control Isn't Just About Work Hours—It's About Energy

Time isn't the only resource you need to protect—your **mental bandwidth** is just as valuable. And if you're always "on," constantly multitasking, or drowning in small tasks, you're draining your energy reserves. The most successful people don't just control their time—they control their **focus.**

This means being intentional about:
Prioritizing high-impact work—focus on what moves the

needle, not what fills the day.

Batching tasks—group similar activities to minimize mental switching.

Taking real breaks—because rest isn't wasted time—it's fuel for better output.

When you master energy management, you're not just more productive—you're more powerful.

Work-Life Control Requires Consistency—Not Perfection

Here's the kicker: you're never going to achieve perfect balance. And that's okay. Work-life control isn't about perfection—it's about consistency. It's about making daily choices that reinforce your priorities and protect your well-being.

Some weeks, work will take more. Other weeks, life will demand your focus. The goal isn't to split your time evenly—it's to stay in the driver's seat. To make decisions from a place of intention, not obligation.

And if you mess up? Recalibrate. Boundaries aren't static—they evolve as your career and life do. The point is to stay conscious and committed to protecting what matters.

No one will hand you control—you have to take it. Here's the bottom line: you are the only person responsible for protecting your time, energy, and life. Waiting for your company or your industry to prioritize your work-life balance is a losing game. The modern workplace isn't designed to care about your well-being—you have to care about it yourself.

But the upside? When you take control, everything changes. You become more effective, less exhausted, and more intentional about the life you're building. And in a world where everyone is constantly overbooked and overstretched, that kind of control isn't just a luxury—it's your greatest advantage.

So forget the balance myth. Aim for control. And don't apologize for protecting your time—because no one else will.

27

The 3-Income Stream Rule

REMOTE WORK PROMISED US LIBERATION. No more long commutes, no more fluorescent-lit cubicles, and no more awkward small talk at the coffee machine. For many, the shift to remote or hybrid work felt like breaking free from the rigid structures of corporate life. Pajamas became the new power suit, and the kitchen table moonlighted as a boardroom. But like most things that sound too good to be true, the reality of remote work is more complex.

Here's the truth: remote work isn't a vacation—it's a different game altogether. And if you want to win at it, you need to master a whole new set of skills. Because while remote work gives you freedom, it also brings unique challenges—staying visible, avoiding burnout, and managing the blurred line between work and home. The difference between thriving remotely and fading into the background lies in how intentionally you approach it.

Out of sight can't mean out of mind—you need to staying visible from afar. One of the biggest risks of remote work is becoming invisible. In a traditional office, your presence alone can signal productivity—you're physically there, people see you working, and casual hallway conversations can shape how others perceive you. But when your office is a Wi-Fi signal, you can't rely on being seen to stay relevant.

If you want to stay visible while working remotely, you have to make your work impossible to ignore. This doesn't mean flooding inboxes or being the loudest voice on Zoom calls—it means being strategic about how you show up.

First, master the art of **proactive communication.** Don't assume people know what you're working on—tell them. Regularly share updates on your progress, insights, and wins. A quick, well-crafted message summarizing key milestones goes a long way in keeping your contributions front and center. You're not bragging—you're ensuring your work doesn't disappear into the digital void.

Second, **show your face.** Video fatigue is real, but turning your camera on during important meetings is a subtle but powerful way to stay present. People connect with faces, not just voices. And while everyone else is hiding behind a blank square, your willingness to be visible reinforces your presence.

Finally, **become the person people trust.** When you deliver consistently—and make it easy for others to rely on you—you build a reputation that transcends physical distance. Be the person who responds quickly (within reason), meets deadlines, and adds value in conversations. Visibility isn't just about being seen—it's about being remembered when opportunities arise.

Why Working from Home Feels Like Working All the Time

Remote work was supposed to bring balance, but for many, it's done the opposite. When your office is also your living room (or bedroom, or kitchen), the boundary between work and rest evaporates. You check emails over breakfast, take meetings from your couch, and suddenly, your entire life feels like one endless workday.

The danger isn't just working more hours—it's never mentally clocking out. When your home becomes your office, your brain never fully switches between "on" and "off." And that low-level hum of constant availability? It's a fast track to burnout.

The solution isn't just working fewer hours—it's creating clear, unbreakable boundaries between work and personal life. Start by establishing a hard stop time every day. Not a vague, "I'll finish when I finish," but a specific time when you shut your laptop and walk away. And mean it.

Physical cues help, too. Designate a specific work zone, even if it's a corner of your apartment. When you're in that zone, you're working—when you leave, work stays behind. This simple mental separation is a game-changer for protecting your personal time.

And here's a radical concept: **turn off notifications.** Unless you're in a life-or-death industry, nothing requires you to be reachable 24/7. Remote work isn't about being constantly available—it's about delivering results. Protect your focus, and your energy will follow.

Location Independence Isn't All Beach Views and Laptop Lattes

Let's talk about the fantasy of remote work—the image of answering emails from a tropical beach, sipping an iced latte while your bank account fills itself. While Instagram may sell you that dream, the reality is messier.

First, **time zones are chaos.** If you're working across multiple regions, your workday might stretch from dawn to dusk. Meetings at odd hours can disrupt your entire rhythm, and collaborating across time zones means constantly negotiating schedules.

Second, **isolation is real.** Working remotely can be lonely—especially if you thrive on in-person energy. There's no casual banter, no impromptu brainstorming sessions, and no Friday happy hours to blow off steam. If you don't actively cultivate human connection, remote work can leave you feeling like you're working on an island.

The fix? **Create structure where none exists.** Maintain a routine that keeps your life grounded—start and end your workday consistently. Schedule virtual (or real-life) coworking sessions with peers to break the isolation. And if you're constantly battling time zones, negotiate for asynchronous work where possible—so you can work on your terms, not someone else's clock.

Negotiate for Remote Perks—Because You Deserve More

Here's the secret most people miss: remote work isn't just about location—it's about leverage. And if your company benefits from your flexibility, you should, too.

When negotiating remote work terms, don't stop at location flexibility. Push for perks that protect your time and mental health. Some ideas:

- **Home office stipends:** Your couch isn't a proper workstation—ask for an allowance to upgrade your setup.
- **Asynchronous hours:** If you're delivering results, do you really need to be "on" from 9 to 5?
- **Mental health days:** Remote work blurs boundaries— extra rest days protect against burnout.

Frame your request around mutual benefit. You're not asking for favors—you're advocating for the conditions that make you more effective. And effective people are worth investing in.

When Home Is the Office—Manage Your Time Like a CEO

Freedom without structure is chaos. When you work remotely, your time is your most valuable asset—and managing it requires discipline.

Start by owning your calendar. Block focused work time where no meetings are allowed. Use these blocks to tackle high-priority tasks without interruption. Guard these slots fiercely—because once they're gone, they're gone.

Batch similar tasks together to avoid context-switching. If you're answering emails all day, you're not actually working—you're reacting. Instead, designate specific times for communication and stick to them.

And most importantly? Schedule your life with as much intention as your work. If you're not careful, remote work will devour your personal time. So, book workouts, coffee dates, or even an hour to read—because if it's not on your calendar, it won't happen.

At its core, remote work is about control. It gives you the power to design a career that fits your life—not the other way around. But that freedom isn't automatic—you have to claim it.

Stay visible by making your work known. Set boundaries that protect your mental health. Advocate for perks that make remote life sustainable. And above all, treat your time like the precious resource it is.

Because the truth is, remote work can be freedom—but only if you do it right.

28

Burnout Isn't a Badge of Honor

SIDE HUSTLES HAVE BECOME THE unofficial currency of ambition. Everywhere you turn, someone's juggling a full-time job while building a business, freelancing on the side, or monetizing their passions. The narrative is seductive: Why settle for one paycheck when you could have multiple? And in a world where job security feels like a relic of the past, who wouldn't want a backup plan (or two)?

But there's a hidden cost nobody talks about—the way side hustles blur the already fragile line between work and life. When your "off hours" are filled with endless to-do lists, client calls, or packaging orders, personal time starts to feel like a luxury you can't afford. If you're not careful, what began as an empowering pursuit of freedom can quickly morph into a relentless cycle where you're always working and rarely living.

Here's the thing: you can chase multiple goals without losing yourself—but only if you balance the tightrope with intention. It's not just about making more money—it's about doing it in a way that doesn't drain your energy or relationships. Because let's be real: if your side hustle burns you out, is it really worth it?

The biggest challenge of balancing a side hustle is that the boundaries between work and life get dangerously thin. When your side gig lives on the same devices you use to unwind—your phone, your laptop—it's easy to slip into a pattern where you're *always* "just checking something." What starts as a quick glance at your inbox during dinner can spiral into three hours of work that hijacks your entire evening.

The solution isn't throwing your side hustle out the window—it's creating hard, non-negotiable boundaries. This means defining when you work on your side hustle—and when you don't. If you let it bleed into every part of your day, it will consume your mental bandwidth and leave nothing for the people and things that matter outside of work.

Start by carving out designated hustle time. Whether it's two focused hours in the evening or early morning sprints before your day job, give your side hustle a structured space. Then, protect the rest of your time fiercely. Just because you *could* work 24/7 doesn't mean you should. Remember: your side hustle exists to enhance your life—not replace it.

Chasing Ambitions Without Losing Relationships

One of the least-talked-about casualties of the side hustle grind? Your relationships. When you're constantly in "build mode," it's easy to deprioritize the people you love—often without realizing it. Missed date nights, distracted conversations, and the constant hum of "I'm busy" can slowly chip away at even the strongest bonds.

But here's the truth: you don't have to choose between your ambitions and your relationships—you just need to be intentional. If you're going to commit to a side hustle, commit to the people you care about, too. Schedule quality time the same way you schedule work time. Block out evenings for family, unplug during dinner, and be fully present when you're together.

And communicate—early and often. Be honest about your

workload and why you're doing it. When your partner, friends, or family understand the bigger picture, they're more likely to support your grind instead of resenting it. But they can't read your mind—you have to tell them.

Knowing When to Push—And When to Pull Back

Not every season is meant for full-speed hustle. Sometimes, scaling back is the smartest move you can make—especially if your side gig is bleeding into every corner of your life. But how do you know when to push harder versus when to slow down?

Start by asking yourself: What's the goal? Is your side hustle about creating freedom? Earning extra cash? Building a business that could eventually replace your day job? If you're grinding without a clear purpose, you'll burn out fast. But if your hustle is aligned with a meaningful goal, you'll know when it's worth pushing through and when it's time to pause.

Another red flag? When the hustle is costing more than it's paying. If you're sacrificing sleep, health, and relationships for a few extra dollars, the math isn't adding up. Side hustles should enhance your life—not deplete it. Don't be afraid to slow down or simplify when you feel your mental and emotional reserves running low. The work will still be there—but you need to protect your capacity to do it.

And sometimes, the right move is automating or outsourcing. If you find yourself drowning in repetitive tasks, invest in tools that can handle the load or hire someone to help. You don't have to do everything yourself—especially if doing everything is slowing your growth.

The Illusion of 24/7 Hustle Culture

We've all seen the glorified version of hustle culture—the idea that working around the clock is a badge of honor. But here's the truth no one tells you: working 24/7 isn't a strategy—it's a trap. If your life revolves around constant productivity, burnout isn't a possibility—it's inevitable.

What's worse? The non-stop hustle often leads to diminishing returns. Your brain wasn't designed to operate at full throttle indefinitely. When you don't rest, your creativity drops, decision fatigue kicks in, and even simple tasks start to feel impossible. Hustling harder isn't the solution—hustling smarter is.

The best side hustlers know that rest is a productivity tool. They don't just schedule work—they schedule recovery. They understand that a refreshed mind does better work in less time. If you're serious about your hustle, get serious about your rest, too. Build "off" days into your schedule where no work happens. Give yourself permission to recharge without guilt.

And don't buy into the myth that your worth is tied to your output. You are not your productivity. You deserve joy, rest, and ease—no matter how ambitious you are.

Balancing Ambition with Actual Life

At the end of the day, the goal isn't to juggle everything perfectly—it's to create a life where both your ambitions and your well-being thrive. You don't have to sacrifice your relationships, mental health, or personal time to chase your goals—but you do have to be intentional.

Start by defining what success really looks like for you. Is it financial freedom? More time with loved ones? A creative outlet that lights you up? Knowing your "why" will help you make better decisions about where to invest your energy.

Set clear boundaries and honor them. Be honest about what you can handle, and don't be afraid to scale back when you need to. Protect your relationships with the same care you give your career. And most importantly—make room for joy.

Your side hustle is just one part of your life—not the whole thing. And when you get the balance right, you'll discover the ultimate reward isn't just the extra income—it's the freedom to live on your own terms.

29

Don't Just Work Hard—Work Visible

IN A WORLD WHERE NOTIFICATIONS never sleep, being "always on" has become the default setting. Emails flood your inbox, Slack pings pull you into endless conversations, and your phone buzzes with updates that somehow always feel urgent. The result? A mind constantly on high alert—fractured, distracted, and exhausted. We tell ourselves that staying connected is the key to productivity, but the truth is, constant digital noise is quietly killing your focus and your career potential.

The modern workplace glorifies being busy—but busy doesn't mean effective. In fact, the more time you spend glued to screens and reacting to endless notifications, the less time you have to engage in the deep, strategic work that moves your career forward. True productivity isn't about doing more—it's about doing what matters. And to do that, you need to reclaim your mental clarity. That's where the digital detox comes in—not as a cute wellness trend, but as a career power move.

Your brain was never designed to process information at the speed of social feeds and inbox overload. Every ping, alert, and pop-up demands a slice of your attention—and that constant context-switching comes with a price. Studies show it takes an average of 23 minutes to regain focus after a distraction. Now multiply that by the hundreds of notifications you encounter daily. It's no wonder you feel perpetually behind.

When your focus is scattered, your ability to think critically, problem-solve, and innovate takes a hit. You may be working longer hours, but you're not working smarter. And while it might feel like you can't afford to unplug, the reality is—you can't afford **not** to.

Digital overload doesn't just sap your mental energy—it hijacks your emotional well-being too. Constant exposure to work messages can blur the boundary between your professional and personal life, leaving you mentally tethered to your job long after you've "clocked out." Over time, this low-grade anxiety creeps into every corner of your life, chipping away at your motivation and increasing your risk of burnout.

Why Unplugging Makes You More Valuable

It sounds counterintuitive, but stepping away from the noise doesn't make you less productive—it makes you more effective. When you reclaim time from the constant barrage of information, you give your brain the space it needs to do its best work.

Think about the people at the top of their game—they're not spending every waking minute checking emails or scrolling through notifications. They prioritize focus and deep thinking. When you create intentional gaps in digital consumption, you sharpen your ability to problem-solve, develop long-term strategies, and outthink the competition.

And here's the kicker: the more valuable your work becomes, the less you have to hustle for recognition. People who bring clear, insightful ideas to the table stand out—not those who are just perpetually available. By prioritizing focused, meaningful work over constant responsiveness, you position yourself as a leader—not just a worker bee.

Practical Strategies to Reduce Digital Overload

The idea of a full digital detox might sound extreme—especially if your career relies on being connected. But you don't need to go off the grid to regain control. Small, intentional changes can create powerful shifts in how you work and live.

Start by **reclaiming your mornings.** Resist the urge to dive straight into emails or social media the moment you wake up. Those first waking hours are when your brain is at its sharpest—protect them for creative thinking or priority tasks.

Batch your notifications. Instead of reacting to every ping in real time, schedule specific windows to check messages. This simple shift reduces context-switching and allows you to stay immersed in important work.

Create **no-phone zones.** Designate specific areas—like your bedroom or dining table—as screen-free zones. This physical separation gives your brain the signal to unwind and recharge.

And here's a bold move: Take a work-free weekend once a month. Completely unplugging for 48 hours resets your mental clarity and creativity in ways that no amount of "hustle" can replicate.

Notifications are designed to be addictive. Every buzz or chime triggers a dopamine hit—pulling you back into an endless loop of checking, scrolling, and refreshing. But that loop steals time from the things that actually matter—your ambitions, your relationships, and your well-being.

To break the cycle, you need to curate your digital environment. Unsubscribe from newsletters you never read. Mute group chats that drain your focus. Disable non-essential notifications across your devices. And—controversial but powerful—turn off email alerts altogether. If something is urgent, people will find a way to reach you.

Take control of your calendar, too. Just because someone invites you to a meeting doesn't mean you're obligated to attend. Protect your deep work time by blocking out focus hours—and treat those blocks as non-negotiable.

The Career Payoff of Digital Minimalism

When you master the art of unplugging, you don't just regain your sanity—you give yourself a strategic advantage. You become the person who thinks ahead while everyone else is drowning in the day-to-day noise.

By creating intentional distance from digital distractions, you'll find yourself making better decisions, delivering higher-quality work, and having the mental bandwidth to spot opportunities others miss. You'll also cultivate a rare skill in the modern world—the ability to focus deeply while everyone else is chasing notifications.

And here's the secret most people miss: When you're intentional about rest, your work accelerates. Detaching from the digital grind gives your brain the recovery time it needs to solve complex problems and generate fresh ideas. You don't need to be available 24/7 to succeed—in fact, setting limits on your availability often makes you more desirable and respected.

There's a myth that being "always on" is a sign of dedication. But the people who truly shape industries and lead movements aren't the ones drowning in their inbox—they're the ones who know when to step back, recharge, and think.

Digital detoxing isn't about rejecting technology—it's about using it on your terms. By creating healthy boundaries around your digital life, you free yourself to focus on what actually drives success: clear thinking, deep work, and intentional action.

So, the next time you feel the pull to check your notifications for the hundredth time, pause. Ask yourself: Is this moving me closer to my goals—or pulling me away from them? Because the most powerful career move you can make isn't just doing more—it's knowing when to unplug, recharge, and come back stronger.

30

Your Career Isn't Linear—And That's Your Advantage

IN A WORLD OBSESSED WITH promotions, titles, and pay raises, there's one form of wealth that's quietly becoming the ultimate flex: control over your time. Forget corner offices and six-figure salaries—being the master of your schedule is the new career power move. Why? Because the ability to decide when, where, and how you work isn't just about convenience—it's about reclaiming your life on your terms.

Time freedom is more than just a trendy buzzword. It's the modern-day currency that separates those trapped in the grind from those designing careers that work for them—not the other way around. When you control your time, you control your energy, your priorities, and ultimately, your success. And here's the thing: you don't need to quit your job or launch a start-up to claim more freedom. The real power lies in knowing how to bend the rules of traditional work without breaking them.

Why Flexibility Is the Ultimate Modern Perk

Let's be real—free snacks and office ping-pong tables aren't cutting it anymore. In a post-pandemic world where remote work proved that productivity isn't tied to a cubicle, flexibility is no longer a luxury—it's an expectation. People want more than a paycheck; they want autonomy. The ability to attend a midday yoga class, pick up their kids without stress, or simply avoid soul-sucking commutes is the new gold standard.

And it's not just about lifestyle perks—flexibility fuels better work. When you're not chained to rigid office hours, you can design your day around your energy peaks and creative rhythms. Imagine knocking out your most important work during your prime focus hours instead of forcing brilliance at 9 a.m. just because a clock says so. The freedom to work when you're naturally most effective makes you sharper, more productive, and—ironically—more valuable to any employer.

The companies that get it? They're winning the talent war. Top performers aren't drawn to old-school models of "butts in seats." They want results-driven environments where output matters more than hours clocked. And if your current job isn't offering that, don't panic—there are ways to negotiate more freedom without handing in your resignation letter.

How to Structure Your Day for Autonomy (Even in Rigid Jobs)

If you're stuck in a traditional 9-to-5, you might think time freedom is out of reach. It's not. The trick is to shift your approach without waving a "down with corporate" flag.

Start by identifying the non-negotiables of your role—what absolutely must get done, and what's just busywork disguised as urgency? When you get clear on your real responsibilities, you can focus on delivering high-impact work while quietly reconfiguring your schedule for more breathing room.

One power move? Own your calendar. Block out your most productive hours for deep work—and fiercely protect that time.

If possible, batch meetings into specific windows rather than scattering them across your day. This reduces context-switching (the enemy of efficiency) and gives you the freedom to control the rest of your schedule.

And don't underestimate the power of proactive communication. Frame your request for flexibility around business outcomes, not personal convenience. Instead of saying, "I want to leave early," try, "I've found that focusing on project work in the mornings with fewer meetings increases my output—would you be open to a trial period where I shift my schedule slightly?" Most managers care about results, not micromanaging your clock.

Designing a Life Where Work Fits Around Your Values

Here's the truth: work is a part of life—not your entire identity. Yet so many people shape their days around job demands instead of their actual priorities. If you don't define your boundaries, someone else will do it for you.

Start by asking yourself: What does an ideal workday look like? Maybe it's starting later so you can take your kids to school. Maybe it's carving out afternoons for personal projects. Or perhaps it's as simple as reclaiming your evenings instead of answering emails at dinner.

Once you know what you want, it's time to align your work around those priorities. This might mean negotiating remote days, adjusting your hours, or shifting to project-based deliverables that give you more autonomy. Remember: freedom isn't given—it's negotiated.

If you're serious about designing a life where work fits around your values, get clear on your "non-negotiables." These are the boundaries you refuse to compromise—whether it's keeping weekends sacred or ensuring no meetings before 10 a.m. When you enforce these limits consistently, you signal that your time is valuable—and that respecting it leads to better work.

How to Negotiate More Freedom Without Quitting

Here's a little secret: most companies have more flexibility than they advertise—you just have to know how to ask for it. And no, you don't need to threaten to quit to make your case.

Start by gathering evidence. If you've been delivering strong results, exceeding expectations, or solving problems independently, you're in a prime position to request more autonomy. When you approach your boss, make it **a win-win proposal.** For example:

- Instead of: "I want to work remotely twice a week,"
- Say: "I've found I'm most productive when working from home—would you be open to a flexible arrangement where I spend two days focused on deep work remotely while remaining fully available for team collaboration?"

By framing your request around how it benefits both you and the company, you're more likely to get a yes. And if your manager hesitates? Suggest a **trial period.** Demonstrate that your output improves with more control over your schedule, and suddenly, your flexibility becomes an asset—not a favour.

Money is great—but without control over your time, even a fat paycheck can feel like a golden cage. The people who thrive in today's unpredictable career landscape are those who prioritize autonomy over rigid definitions of success.

When you control your time, you're no longer at the mercy of burnout cycles or toxic "always-on" cultures. You can invest energy where it matters most—whether that's building a side hustle, spending time with loved ones, or pursuing personal growth. And paradoxically, the more you assert control over your schedule, the **more valuable you become** to organizations that prioritize innovation and independent thinking.

The ultimate career flex isn't working 80 hours a week—it's having the freedom to choose **when and how you work** while still delivering results that move the needle. So, stop waiting for permission to reclaim your time. Whether you're in a corporate role, freelancing, or building your empire, the power to design a life on your terms is already within reach. The only question is—are you ready to take it?

PART 7

Take Control—Because No One Else Will

31

Own Your Time—Or Someone Else Will

ONCE UPON A TIME, AMBITION meant climbing the corporate ladder—one rung at a time. You picked a career path, stuck to it, and if you worked hard enough, success followed in a straight line. Fast-forward to today, and that ladder? It's more like a jungle gym. The people winning now aren't just the smartest or the hardest-working—they're the ones who can pivot, stretch, and reinvent themselves on demand. In a world where industries can be disrupted overnight, adaptability isn't a bonus trait—it's the survival skill that separates those who thrive from those who fade into irrelevance.

Here's the reality check: Your degree, your job title, and your current skill set have an expiration date. The world is moving too fast to cling to outdated career identities. Automation, AI, and new technologies are rewriting the rules of work, and if you're still playing by last decade's playbook, you're already behind. Being adaptable means staying ahead—not just reacting when change hits, but anticipating it and positioning yourself to benefit.

The old-school ambition that says, "Stick to the plan, and you'll be rewarded"? It doesn't work anymore. Modern ambition looks like constant evolution—being bold enough to step out of your comfort zone and sharp enough to recognize when it's time to switch gears. The people shaping the future know that clinging to one career script is a losing game. Adaptability isn't just about survival—it's about seizing opportunities that others are too rigid to notice.

Let's talk facts—AI is changing everything. Tasks that once required human skill are being automated at lightning speed. But while AI can analyze data, write reports, and even create content, it can't replace human adaptability. The ability to navigate ambiguity, connect ideas across disciplines, and pivot when the ground shifts—that's a uniquely human advantage. And in a tech-dominated future, it's your most valuable asset.

Raw talent used to be enough to stand out. Not anymore. You can be a genius at what you do, but if you can't adapt to new technologies or shifting demands, you'll quickly become obsolete. What separates future-proof professionals from everyone else is their willingness to learn, unlearn, and relearn—on repeat.

And here's the kicker: adaptability isn't just about surviving disruption—it's about capitalizing on it. When entire industries are transforming, new gaps open up for those quick enough to spot them. The people who stay curious and flexible will always be first in line for emerging opportunities, while those clinging to "the way things have always been" will be left scrambling.

How to Embrace Career Changes as Opportunities

If the thought of career change makes you anxious, you're not alone. Humans are wired to seek stability—it's why most people avoid change until it's forced on them. But here's the thing: Every career pivot is a chance to level up—if you're willing to play offense instead of defense.

The key is shifting your mindset from threat to opportunity.

Instead of seeing disruption as a career-ending disaster, frame it as a launchpad for reinvention. Every change—whether it's a layoff, a new technology, or a shifting industry—carries hidden opportunities for those willing to explore new possibilities.

Start by asking: What's the next skill or knowledge gap I can fill? Don't wait until your job is on the line—actively seek out the trends shaping your field. Follow the innovators, dive into new tools, and build skills that make you indispensable. The people who adapt quickly aren't afraid to experiment. They take risks, try new roles, and understand that every pivot is a stepping stone—not a setback.

And when you do pivot? Leverage your existing experience. Too many people think starting over means erasing the past. Wrong. Your current skills are a launchpad, not a liability. Whether you're transitioning industries or shifting job functions, your unique perspective is an asset that can differentiate you in new arenas.

Building a Mindset That Thrives in Uncertainty

Adaptable people aren't just good at learning new skills—they're mentally tough. They know that uncertainty is a constant, and instead of resisting it, they lean in. Cultivating that mindset starts with reframing uncertainty as a challenge to grow, not a threat to fear.

One way to build adaptability muscle? Get comfortable being uncomfortable. Stretch yourself regularly—whether it's taking on unfamiliar projects, working with diverse teams, or learning outside your expertise. The more you expose yourself to unfamiliar terrain, the more resilient and adaptable you become.

And don't underestimate the power of curiosity. People who stay curious—who ask better questions and chase new knowledge—are better equipped to handle rapid change. When you approach your career with a learner's mindset, every shift becomes a chance to grow stronger.

The Habits of Hyper-Adaptable Professionals

Adaptable professionals have a playbook—whether they know it or not. Their careers don't follow linear paths, but they consistently stay ahead of the curve. Here's how:

They treat learning as a lifestyle. They don't just learn when they have to—they're constantly seeking new ideas, skills, and trends. Podcasts, online courses, industry events—these aren't optional extras. They're non-negotiables.

They experiment without fear. Hyper-adaptable people test new waters without needing everything to be perfect. Whether it's launching a side project, shifting roles, or adopting new tech, they view experimentation as a way to future-proof themselves.

They build diverse networks. Staying adaptable isn't just about knowledge—it's about who you know. The most agile professionals maintain relationships across industries because they understand that career pivots often happen through unexpected connections.

They stay open to reinvention. Adaptability means being willing to evolve. If their current identity no longer fits the world around them, they don't cling to it—they embrace reinvention as part of the process.

Here's the million-dollar question: Can you pivot without losing the traction you've already built? Absolutely—if you're strategic about it. The key is to view pivots as an expansion of your career, not a break from it.

When pivoting, focus on bridging your past and future. Identify transferable skills that apply to your new direction and frame your transition around the value you bring. Employers and clients care less about your exact experience and more about how you can solve problems in new contexts.

And while pivoting requires bold moves, don't burn bridges. Keep relationships strong, even as you shift gears. Your past network is a goldmine for future opportunities—whether it's advice, referrals, or collaborations.

Ultimately, adaptability is the new ambition because the most successful careers aren't defined by rigid goals—they're shaped by a willingness to evolve. In a world where change is the only constant, your ability to pivot is your greatest competitive advantage. Embrace it, and you won't just survive the future—you'll shape it.

32

Learn Fast, Adapt Faster—The Only Real Job Security

IF THERE'S ONE TRUTH ABOUT modern careers, it's this: Staying still is the fastest way to fall behind. In a world where technology evolves overnight and job descriptions change faster than your LinkedIn headline, the people who win aren't the ones with the most impressive résumés—they're the ones who never stop learning. Forget job security through loyalty. Your real career insurance is your ability to keep growing, adapting, and upskilling—no matter how far along you are.

The old model of learning—study hard, get a degree, and ride that wave for 40 years—has expired. In its place is a new reality where skills depreciate like smartphones. What was cutting-edge five years ago is already old news, and the only way to stay ahead is to make learning an ongoing, intentional practice. In short? If you're not constantly upgrading yourself, you're becoming obsolete.

But here's the good news: The people who commit to lifelong learning hold all the cards. When industries shift, they're the first to pivot. When new opportunities emerge, they're ready to grab them. And when automation starts swallowing jobs whole, they're the ones designing the future—not being left behind by it. Lifelong learning isn't just a feel-good concept—it's a survival strategy. And the sooner you embrace it, the more control you'll have over your career trajectory.

Why Constant Upskilling Is the Only Way to Stay Relevant

Here's the harsh reality—your degree is not a golden ticket anymore. With AI automating everything from data analysis to creative writing, what you learned a decade ago won't cut it today. According to research, the half-life of professional skills is shrinking rapidly—what you master now could be outdated in five years or less.

The question is no longer, *"Do I need to keep learning?"* It's *"How fast can I learn, and what's next?"* Upskilling isn't optional—it's the currency of modern careers. Those who consistently invest in expanding their knowledge will stay marketable and ahead of the curve, while those clinging to outdated expertise will find themselves on the sidelines.

But this goes beyond technical skills. Emotional intelligence, leadership, and adaptability—these "soft" skills are becoming harder to automate and more valuable to employers. Staying relevant means developing both the hard skills to perform and the human skills to lead. The workforce is evolving, and if you're not learning alongside it, you're falling behind.

How to Learn New Skills While Working Full-Time

Let's be real—no one has endless free hours to dive into textbooks while juggling a career. But that's not an excuse to stagnate. The most successful people don't find time—they make it. And the trick isn't to overhaul your life; it's to integrate learning seamlessly into your day-to-day.

Start by identifying your learning gaps. What's the next big thing in your industry? What skills are in demand that you don't yet have? Prioritize these areas and break them down into bite-sized learning goals. You don't need to master everything overnight—consistency matters more than intensity.

Use the time you already have. Commutes, lunch breaks, or even 15 minutes before bed can become your personal learning labs. Podcasts, audiobooks, and short video courses make it easier than ever to turn dead time into development time. And if you're stuck in meetings all day, consider habit-stacking—pairing learning with something you already do. Listening to an industry podcast while you work out? That's a power move.

And here's a bonus: Get your employer to pay for it. Many companies offer tuition reimbursement, access to professional development programs, or internal training. Don't leave that benefit on the table—use it to fund your growth while sharpening your edge.

The Best (and Fastest) Ways to Future-Proof Yourself

If you want to stay ahead, you need a strategy—not random bursts of learning. The best learners in today's job market are deliberate about what they study and why. Here's how to future-proof yourself while moving fast:

Follow the trends—not the crowd. Instead of chasing every new fad, focus on skills that are consistently rising in value. AI literacy, digital marketing, data analytics, and strategic thinking—these competencies have staying power across industries.

Invest in cross-functional skills. It's not enough to be good at one thing anymore. The most valuable professionals can connect dots across disciplines. If you're in marketing, learn data science basics. If you're in tech, sharpen your communication skills. This kind of T-shaped knowledge (deep in one area, broad across others) makes you indispensable.

Learn in public. Document your learning journey through blogs, LinkedIn posts, or personal projects. Not only does this reinforce your knowledge—it also signals your growth to future employers and collaborators.

Be an early adopter. Pay attention to emerging technologies and industry shifts. Being the first in your company to master a new tool or process gives you leverage and positions you as a go-to expert.

If traditional learning feels too time-consuming, micro-learning is your new best friend. Instead of blocking off hours for coursework, micro-learning focuses on quick, high-impact learning bursts. And guess what? It works. Studies show that we retain information better when we absorb it in short, frequent intervals.

Think of it as **snackable education.** Five-minute tutorials, 10-minute case studies, or quick deep-dives on platforms like LinkedIn Learning, Coursera, and YouTube can fit into even the busiest schedule. When done consistently, these micro-moments compound into serious knowledge over time.

The secret? **Make it a habit.** Instead of waiting for a quiet weekend to dive into learning, incorporate micro-learning into your daily rhythm. Set a rule: **Learn something new every day.** It could be a fresh framework, a new tech tool, or a business insight—small, steady learning pays massive long-term dividends.

How to Stay Curious in an Ever-Changing Job Market

Curiosity isn't a nice-to-have—it's the engine that drives lifelong learning. The most adaptable people are relentlessly curious. They don't just ask, "How does this work?"—they ask, "What comes next?"

To stay curious, surround yourself with inspiration. Follow thought leaders in your industry, subscribe to future-focused newsletters, and stay plugged into conversations shaping your field. When you stay informed, curiosity becomes second nature.

And don't be afraid to explore outside your lane. Some of the best career insights come from unexpected places. A designer learning data analytics. A coder studying psychology. The more diverse your knowledge base, the more creative and adaptable you become.

Curiosity also thrives on community. Connect with people who challenge your thinking—whether through mastermind groups, industry events, or online forums. Being around ambitious, forward-thinking people keeps your intellectual appetite sharp.

At the end of the day, your career is only as resilient as your ability to keep learning. In a world where nothing stays the same for long, lifelong learning isn't just an advantage—it's your most powerful insurance policy against irrelevance.

The question isn't whether you should keep learning—it's whether you can afford not to.

33

From Employee to Entrepreneur—Without Losing Your Mind

FOR DECADES, SUCCESS WAS SOLD as a straight line—pick a career, climb the ladder, retire with a pension. But that script is outdated. Linear careers don't reflect the messy, dynamic reality of the modern workforce. Industries shift overnight, technology disrupts entire fields, and job security is more myth than promise. The people thriving today aren't the ones clinging to a single path—they're the ones willing to pivot. Career pivots aren't signs of confusion; they're power moves. They represent adaptability, ambition, and the ability to evolve while everyone else stays stuck.

The world rewards people who can switch lanes without losing momentum. And here's the truth: you don't have to start from scratch to pivot successfully. Every skill, every experience, and every connection you've built is leverage—even if you're shifting into a seemingly unrelated industry. People often think a career pivot means leaving everything behind, but it's really about repositioning yourself. The best pivots use what you already know in new contexts. That's how you turn your past into your greatest asset.

The key to pivoting is recognizing that your skill set is broader than any single job description. Technical skills are valuable, but it's your transferable abilities—communication, problem-solving, leadership, creativity—that open doors across industries. For instance, someone working in marketing already understands consumer psychology, data analysis, and storytelling. Those same skills apply whether you're marketing sneakers or software. If you're a project manager, you know how to organize complex tasks, manage stakeholders, and deliver results—skills that are invaluable whether you work in tech, healthcare, or finance.

A successful pivot starts with reframing your story. Instead of focusing on where you've been, focus on where you're going—and how your experience makes you the ideal person to get there. Your résumé and LinkedIn shouldn't read like a disconnected series of jobs. They should tell a cohesive narrative: "I've solved these kinds of problems, and now I'm ready to solve them in a new way." It's not about erasing your past—it's about translating it.

The emotional side of career pivots is real, though. Change brings uncertainty, and stepping into the unknown can feel like losing your professional identity. But here's the thing—your identity isn't tied to a job title. It's tied to the value you create. People get stuck because they mistake familiarity for security. But staying in a job that no longer excites or challenges you isn't safe—it's a slow path to irrelevance. The most successful people aren't immune to fear; they just refuse to let it keep them in places they've outgrown.

Imposter syndrome also loves to show up during pivots. You might wonder if you're "qualified enough" or if people will take you seriously. The secret? Most people are making it up as they go. Confidence isn't the prerequisite for pivoting—it's the result of doing it. No one feels 100% ready to jump industries or reinvent themselves. But you become qualified by stepping in, showing up, and figuring it out. Growth always happens outside your comfort zone. If you're not a little scared, you're probably playing too small.

Real career pivots aren't just about chasing new opportunities—they're about escaping old limitations. People who pivot well understand that job titles are temporary, but their ability to create value is permanent. And sometimes, pivoting isn't about abandoning a career—it's about expanding it. You can move horizontally into new departments, explore interdisciplinary roles, or layer side projects on top of your main gig. You're not boxed in by a single path unless you choose to be.

Take, for example, the former schoolteacher who pivoted into corporate learning and development. Her ability to break down complex concepts and engage learners was invaluable in a business setting. Or the journalist who shifted into tech communications—turning years of storytelling into a powerful tool for brand messaging. These weren't people with linear résumés. They were people who understood how to leverage their past while embracing the future.

Pivots aren't always smooth, but they are always worth it. At first, you might face rejection from people who can't see past your last job. That's fine. You're not for everyone. What matters is that you know how to position yourself clearly and confidently. If you're switching industries, build a bridge with your existing skills. If you're stepping into a new role, start learning the language of that space. Talk to people doing the work you want to do. Your network is your shortcut—use it. Informational interviews, mentorship, and industry events are goldmines for pivoters.

Another power move? Create proof of work. In a world where everyone's résumé looks the same, showing beats telling. Write about your ideas. Build a small project that demonstrates your skills. Share your insights online. Employers aren't just hiring based on what you've done—they're hiring based on what they believe you can do next. And nothing makes them believe like seeing your ideas in action.

Timing your pivot matters too. Sometimes you outgrow a job long before you're ready to leave. The best time to start preparing isn't when you're desperate—it's when you're still comfortable. Build new skills on the side. Explore your curiosity. Set up conversations with people in fields you admire. You never want to be in a position where you need to pivot but have no idea where to go next. Career agility is about staying one step ahead.

The most exciting part? Pivots unlock possibilities you can't even imagine from where you are now. The job you think you want might just be a stepping stone to something even bigger. And in a world that's constantly changing, the ability to pivot isn't just a career strategy—it's a survival skill. Linear paths are fragile. Adaptability is unbreakable.

So, if you feel restless, stuck, or like your current job is no longer the right fit—trust that instinct. It's not a sign of failure. It's a signal that you're ready for more. Embrace the pivot. It's not the end of your story—it's how you write your next chapter.

34

Digital Clout Won't Pay Rent— Strategic Moves Will

THE FUTURE OF WORK ISN'T coming—it's already here, and it's moving faster than anyone predicted. Industries rise and fall in the blink of an eye, and the jobs people swore were "safe" are being reshaped by algorithms, automation, and artificial intelligence. The question isn't whether things will change—it's whether you're ready to keep up. Future-proofing your career isn't about locking yourself into a "stable" job and hoping for the best. It's about staying ahead of the curve, developing skills that adapt to change, and knowing where the world is moving before everyone else catches on.

The truth is, the jobs that will dominate the next decade probably don't even exist yet. Entire industries are being built from scratch, fueled by advancements in AI, biotechnology, renewable energy, and digital economies. But while technology is transforming the landscape, there's one thing machines still can't do—be human. The careers that will survive (and thrive) in this new era are the ones that blend technical know-how with deeply human capabilities—empathy, creativity, problem-solving, and adaptability. You're not just future-proofing for machines— you're future-proofing against irrelevance.

One of the clearest signs of where the world is heading lies in emerging industries. From climate tech to virtual reality, new fields are shaping the future economy in ways most people don't even see coming. Renewable energy is surging as governments and corporations pivot toward sustainable solutions. The creator economy is transforming hobbies into multi-million-dollar businesses. Cybersecurity is no longer just a tech concern—it's a global priority as digital spaces become the new battleground. And AI? It's not replacing humans—it's enhancing those who know how to work with it. The real winners are the people who can merge human insight with technological innovation.

Spotting opportunities in disruptive fields isn't about chasing every shiny new industry. It's about recognizing patterns. Whenever a new technology reshapes how we live and work, it creates gaps—new problems to solve, new systems to build, and new expertise to develop. Those who see the gaps first gain a massive advantage. If you want to future-proof your career, start paying attention to where the friction is. Every inefficiency, every complaint, every "this could be better" moment in emerging industries is a window into a future job or business opportunity. The most valuable careers aren't in maintaining the status quo— they're in fixing what's broken and building what's next.

The key to staying relevant is focusing on roles that technology can't easily replace. AI may be able to generate content, but it can't tell a nuanced story the way a human can. Algorithms can crunch data, but they can't interpret its emotional and social implications. Any job that relies purely on repetitive tasks is at risk—but the work that requires human judgment, ethical reasoning, and emotional intelligence will only grow in value. Leadership, relationship-building, and creative strategy are irreplaceable skills in an age of automation. Machines can process—humans can lead. And that difference will define who stays employed and who doesn't.

Transferable skills are the secret weapon for long-term career security. Instead of locking yourself into narrow expertise, invest in skills that carry across industries. Critical thinking, communication, adaptability, and digital literacy will be valuable no matter where the world moves. The more you can pivot those skills to meet the needs of new industries, the more you'll future-proof yourself. For example, the ability to lead remote teams isn't just a pandemic-era necessity—it's becoming a core competency for global businesses. Understanding data is no longer exclusive to tech roles—data fluency is becoming the language of decision-making across every sector.

But here's the thing—staying future-proof isn't just about technical know-how. It's about how you think. Curiosity is the ultimate form of career security. People who stop learning, stop growing. And in a world where the knowledge shelf-life is shrinking, intellectual curiosity isn't a luxury—it's a survival skill. Those who constantly ask, "What's next?" are the ones who stay ahead. Curiosity keeps you adaptable, keeps you connected to evolving industries, and keeps you from becoming obsolete. If you want to thrive in the future, you need to stay relentlessly curious—about people, about systems, and about what's on the horizon.

The people who future-proof their careers aren't waiting for the world to hand them a roadmap. They're creating their own. They watch how industries shift, and they move early. They invest in their own development—not just through formal education but through real-world experience, constant learning, and surrounding themselves with people who push them to think bigger. They don't cling to old identities—they evolve with the world.

And here's the truth no one tells you: Future-proofing isn't about job security—it's about freedom. When you have the skills and the mindset to pivot, you're not trapped by a single job title or industry. You have options. You can walk away from toxic workplaces. You can chase new opportunities without fear. You can build a career that fits your life—not the other way around.

The future is coming fast—but you don't have to be afraid of it. You just have to be ready.

35

You Don't Owe Companies Loyalty

ECONOMIC SHIFTS DON'T JUST RATTLE stock markets—they redefine job security. What felt stable yesterday can become fragile overnight, and no one is immune to the ripple effects. In a world where industries evolve faster than your morning news cycle, relying on a single paycheck is the modern-day equivalent of walking a tightrope without a safety net. The professionals who thrive during recessions aren't the ones clinging to old models—they're the ones who adapt, anticipate, and play the long game. If you want career security when the economy starts shaking, you need to move differently.

The first truth of recession-proofing your career? Job security isn't about keeping a position—it's about staying valuable. Economic downturns force companies to make tough calls, and when budgets shrink, only the indispensable stay. Being valuable isn't just about working harder—it's about working smarter and proving your impact. Are you the person who solves problems, drives results, and makes life easier for your team? If the answer is yes, you become harder to cut. If the answer is no, you're at risk. In tight economies, the people who deliver tangible value always have options.

But value alone won't protect you—you also need visibility. Quiet competence might feel noble, but it's risky. If no one knows the work you're doing, it's easier for decision-makers to overlook you. You don't need to be the loudest person in the room, but you do need to be strategic about showcasing your contributions. Keep a running list of your wins—projects completed, revenue generated, problems solved—and make sure the right people know about them. It's not bragging; it's survival. In uncertain times, visibility equals security.

Staying employable also means staying ahead of the curve. When recessions hit, industries don't just shrink—some transform entirely. The skills that made you valuable last year won't necessarily make you valuable tomorrow. Pay attention to where your field is going. What technologies are emerging? What skills are becoming non-negotiable? If you're in a vulnerable industry, it's time to diversify. Learn new skills before you need them. Certifications, micro-learning platforms, and industry conferences aren't just career boosters—they're career insurance.

A critical but often overlooked move? Build relationships before you need them. The people who bounce back fastest after layoffs aren't the ones mass-applying online—they're the ones who have a strong network. During economic uncertainty, your relationships are your safety net. Invest in your professional circle now. Stay connected with former colleagues, mentors, and industry peers. Engage meaningfully—don't just reach out when you're in trouble. Strong networks open doors when official channels close.

Another recession-proof strategy is recognizing the difference between "safe" and "risky" industries. No job is entirely immune to economic shifts, but some sectors weather storms better than others. Healthcare, technology, education, and essential services tend to remain stable because they address fundamental needs. Meanwhile, luxury markets, non-essential consumer goods, and early-stage startups often take the hardest hits. Pay attention to the industries thriving when others are struggling. If your current field feels unstable, start exploring industries with long-term resilience.

Beyond industry trends, look for companies with solid financial foundations. During downturns, cash flow is king. Companies with strong reserves, diversified revenue streams, and low debt are more likely to retain staff during tough times. If you're considering a job move, research a company's financial health—public filings, industry reports, and even employee reviews can offer valuable clues. It's not just about what the company does—it's about whether they can survive the next storm.

But let's get real: the ultimate form of career security is not relying on a single income stream. The days of one job providing lifelong stability are over. If you're serious about protecting your future, you need multiple streams of income. Side hustles, freelance work, consulting gigs—these aren't just trendy buzzwords; they're lifelines. Even small additional income can cushion you during a layoff. Plus, when you own part of your income, no single employer controls your entire financial fate.

Building multiple income streams doesn't mean burning yourself out. It means being strategic. Start by leveraging your existing skills. If you're a designer, take on freelance projects. If you're a marketing expert, offer consulting services. Turn your knowledge into digital products, courses, or even passive income streams. The goal isn't to add more hours—it's to create smart revenue channels that work while you sleep.

And here's a powerful mindset shift: treat your career like an asset—not just a job. In volatile economies, you can't afford to be passive. Regularly audit your professional life. What skills are growing stale? Which relationships need nurturing? What opportunities are you missing? Just like investors diversify their portfolios, you need to diversify your professional identity. Be someone who can wear multiple hats. If one door closes, you should already have three more cracked open.

Recession-proofing also involves building a financial cushion—because when economies wobble, liquidity is power. Aim to have at least three to six months of living expenses saved. This isn't just about surviving a job loss—it's about giving yourself the freedom to make smart career moves. When you're financially stable, you negotiate better, pivot confidently, and avoid desperation-driven decisions.

And let's not forget the emotional side of job insecurity. Recessions can mess with your head—especially if layoffs happen around you. It's easy to internalize economic forces as personal failure, but don't fall into that trap. Job losses during downturns are rarely about your worth—they're about market realities. Maintaining mental resilience is just as important as building career resilience. If you face a setback, treat it as data—not a death sentence. What can you learn? What opportunities does it open? Every closed door redirects you somewhere new.

The future belongs to the agile—not the anchored. If you want to stay recession-proof, cultivate adaptability as your core skill. Stay curious. Stay connected. Stay ready to pivot. Because in an unpredictable world, the people who move with the tide—not against it—are the ones who come out on top.

The Chaos-Proof Mindset—
Stay Ahead,
Stay Unstoppable

36

Forget the Five-Year Plan—Think Five Moves Ahead

CHASING JOB TITLES IS THE corporate version of a hamster wheel—it looks like progress but often leaves you stuck in place. Sure, fancy titles sound impressive at dinner parties and on LinkedIn, but here's the truth: titles fade, and impact lasts. In a world where industries evolve overnight and AI is creeping into every workflow, the real power move isn't climbing a corporate ladder—it's creating work that actually matters. If your career is just a collection of promotions without purpose, it's easy to lose the plot. The professionals who shape the future are the ones who focus on the value they deliver—not the shiny label attached to their email signature.

Impact outlasts promotions because, at the end of the day, what you do matters more than what you're called. A title is fragile—it's handed to you by an employer and can be taken away just as fast. But the skills you develop, the problems you solve, and the people you influence? Those stay with you. The market rewards people who create undeniable value. Companies will always find room for people who deliver solutions, drive innovation, and make life easier. If you spend your career chasing the next rung on the ladder, you might miss the bigger opportunity: becoming the person no one wants to lose.

So, how do you shift from title-chasing to impact-making? It starts by defining what success means on your terms—not someone else's corporate script. What kind of work lights you up? What problems do you want to solve? What legacy do you want to leave behind? This isn't about five-year plans and vision boards—it's about getting clear on the kind of impact you want to have and making decisions that align with that vision. People who play the long game know that career satisfaction doesn't come from collecting titles; it comes from doing work that aligns with their values and leaves a mark.

Defining your career legacy doesn't mean waiting until you're at the top—it starts now. Every project, every conversation, and every decision is part of the story you're building. Are you just ticking boxes, or are you leaving a real impression? Legacy isn't about ego—it's about intention. Do you want to be known as someone who plays it safe and follows the rules? Or do you want to be the person who questions the status quo, builds new systems, and makes a difference? People who focus on legacy know that every career move is an investment in their future self.

And here's the twist: meaningful work isn't a luxury—it's a survival strategy in chaotic times. When industries shift and job descriptions blur, the people who thrive are those who anchor themselves in purpose. It's easy to burn out when your work feels hollow. But when your work feels meaningful, you become more resilient, creative, and motivated. This doesn't mean quitting your job to "follow your bliss"—it means finding ways to align your daily work with something that matters. Whether it's mentoring a colleague, driving innovation, or serving your community, impact-driven professionals bring energy and vision that titles alone can't provide.

A major shift happens when you stop seeing yourself as a job seeker and start seeing yourself as a value creator. Job seekers wait for opportunities—value creators make them. Titles are given—impact is built. Value creators don't just clock in and out—they identify problems and solve them. They understand that career security doesn't come from a job title—it comes from being the person who delivers results. And when you deliver real results, you gain leverage. You negotiate better salaries, open new doors, and become the kind of professional people want to work with and learn from.

Being a value creator also means playing offense, not defense. Defense is waiting for promotions and hoping your manager notices your work. Offense is building relationships, pitching bold ideas, and taking ownership of your growth. It's about being proactive in shaping your career instead of reacting to what's handed to you. This mindset makes you indispensable. When you focus on solving problems, driving outcomes, and making life easier for those around you, you shift from being another employee to being a force companies can't afford to lose.

Of course, impact isn't just about what you do—it's about who you uplift along the way. Real career power comes from building others up, not just climbing higher yourself. The professionals who leave the biggest marks are those who create opportunities for others, share knowledge generously, and build communities of support. This isn't just altruism—it's smart strategy. When you invest in people, you build a network of advocates who root for your success. Your career will stretch decades—do you want to spend it competing in a zero-sum game, or do you want to create a legacy where everyone wins?

And let's be honest—chasing titles often comes with a hidden cost. The pressure to constantly level up can pull you away from what actually matters. Promotions can mean longer hours, more stress, and less time for the things you love. Titles won't comfort you when you're burnt out at midnight, wondering why your life revolves around performance reviews. The deeper reward comes from knowing your work is meaningful—whether or not there's a VP title attached to it. When you chase impact, you redefine success on your terms.

So, how do you know if you're chasing a title or chasing impact? Ask yourself this: if the title disappeared tomorrow, would the work still matter to you? If the answer is no, you're likely on the wrong path. If the answer is yes, you're already ahead of the game. Impact isn't about flashy labels or corporate accolades—it's about knowing you're leaving the world better than you found it. When you focus on impact, you build a career that outlasts any title. The bottom line? Titles may open doors—but impact breaks them down. While everyone else is chasing the next big promotion, play a smarter game. Focus on the work that matters, deliver undeniable value, and lift others as you climb. Because in the long run, titles fade—but the impact you leave behind? That's forever.

37

Confidence Is Currency

IN A WORLD OBSESSED WITH instant results and quick wins, career capital is the slow-burn advantage no one talks about—but it's the difference between begging for opportunities and having them chase you. Career capital isn't just about the years you've worked or the titles you've held; it's the rare, valuable skills and deep expertise you accumulate over time. It's the kind of leverage that puts you in rooms where decisions are made and gives you the power to write your own career script. When you invest in building career capital, you stop relying on job applications and start moving through the world with undeniable value.

Think of career capital as your personal bank of skills, knowledge, and networks—assets that no employer can take away from you. Job titles are temporary, but career capital is permanent. It's the thing that makes your name come up in closed-door meetings when new opportunities arise. It's the reason you get headhunted instead of sending out résumés. The people who dominate in any industry aren't the ones with the flashiest titles—they're the ones with the deepest wells of skill and expertise. When you cultivate career capital, you future-proof yourself against layoffs, industry shifts, and even economic downturns.

The key to building career capital is focusing on rare and valuable skills—the kind of abilities that not everyone can offer.

These aren't just technical skills (although those are valuable); they're also strategic thinking, leadership, and problem-solving. Anyone can learn the basics, but true career capital comes from becoming exceptional at things that are both useful and hard to replicate. The market rewards those who can do what others can't—or won't. If your skill set is easily replaceable, so is your position. But if you're the person who delivers solutions no one else can, you become indispensable.

Developing these skills isn't about waiting for your manager to hand you a development plan. It's about taking ownership of your growth. You build career capital by going beyond your job description—taking on stretch projects, diving into new technologies, and solving complex problems others avoid. It's in the extra work most people are too lazy or too scared to touch. And it's not just about doing more—it's about doing smarter. Identify the skills that are both rare and in demand, and invest time into mastering them. This isn't about checking off boxes for a performance review; it's about turning yourself into a powerhouse.

And here's the game-changer: career capital isn't just about technical mastery—it's also about the experiences that shape how you think and lead. The ability to navigate ambiguity, influence stakeholders, and drive outcomes is just as valuable as technical know-how. This is the kind of capital that transcends industries. When you know how to solve hard problems, you can pivot into new spaces without starting from scratch. The more you stretch yourself into uncomfortable situations—whether it's leading a crisis response or launching a new initiative—the more career capital you bank.

Leveraging career capital is where things get really interesting. The more value you accumulate, the more control you have over your career moves. People with deep career capital don't wait for permission—they shape their own paths. This is where negotiation power comes into play. When you bring rare, undeniable skills to the table, you're not just another candidate—you're an asset. Companies know they can't afford to lose people with real capital, which means you have leverage to negotiate higher pay, better roles, and more freedom. And here's the truth: companies always have more budget and flexibility than they admit—but only for people who bring serious value.

When you're negotiating from a place of strength, everything shifts. You can push for things beyond salary—equity, remote work, professional development, and creative control. But you only get this kind of leverage when your career capital makes you hard to replace. Average employees negotiate for breadcrumbs; people with career capital negotiate the whole table. The difference? One waits to be chosen, the other chooses. And career capital is what tips the balance in your favour.

Another major advantage of building career capital is how it opens doors to future opportunities—often before you even know you want them. When you're exceptional at what you do, word travels. Your network becomes stronger because people trust your expertise. Decision-makers start reaching out with offers because your reputation precedes you. This is how people land dream jobs without ever applying—because their career capital does the talking. And the best part? The more you invest in building capital now, the easier it becomes to pivot later.

But here's what no one tells you—building career capital isn't always glamorous. It requires patience and long-term thinking. It means playing the game strategically instead of chasing every shiny opportunity. It means doing the hard, sometimes invisible work when no one's watching. The payoff, though, is that once you have career capital, you have options. And in a volatile job market, options are everything. When you're in demand, you're not worried about layoffs or industry shake-ups—you're deciding where you want to go next.

If you want to future-proof your career, your primary focus should be on growing and protecting your capital. This means constantly sharpening your skills, expanding your knowledge, and staying curious. It also means documenting your wins—because your career capital is only as strong as your ability to communicate it. Keep track of the major problems you've solved, the innovations you've driven, and the results you've delivered. When the time comes to leverage your capital, you need the receipts.

And here's the real flex: people with career capital play a different game altogether. While others worry about job security, you're building long-term autonomy. You're not just climbing a corporate ladder—you're building your own empire, skill by skill. Career capital is the ultimate cheat code because it lets you design a career on your own terms. Titles fade, industries evolve, but capital? That's forever. When you invest in your own value, you stop chasing jobs—and start building a career that works for you.

38

The Art of Staying Relevant

IN A WORLD OBSESSED WITH quick wins and instant gratification, the long game mindset is an unfair advantage. It's the difference between people who bounce from job to job, always chasing the next shiny thing, and those who build careers that stand the test of time. Playing the long game means thinking beyond your next paycheck, promotion, or performance review. It's about making moves today that set you up for power, freedom, and opportunities years down the line. And while everyone else is busy hacking their way to overnight success, you're building something that lasts.

Long-term thinkers understand that today's decisions shape tomorrow's possibilities. It's easy to get caught up in the urgency of now—chasing every trend, saying yes to every opportunity, and reacting to whatever pops up next. But here's the truth: not every move is worth your energy. When you adopt a long game mindset, you shift from reacting to strategizing. You start making decisions with your future self in mind—what you do now isn't just about this year's goals but about where you want to be in five, ten, or even twenty years. That kind of thinking separates people who merely survive from those who thrive.

One of the most powerful things about the long game mindset is how it compounds over time. Small, smart moves—consistently made—stack up in ways that people playing the short game can't see. This isn't just about huge career leaps. It's about planting seeds today that quietly grow until, one day, they become impossible to ignore. Whether it's developing a niche skill, building genuine professional relationships, or establishing your personal brand, these efforts might seem small now—but in the long run, they become your greatest assets. The people who seem to "suddenly" succeed? They were playing the long game while everyone else was looking for shortcuts.

But here's the twist—playing the long game doesn't mean rejecting short-term wins. You need both. The key is learning how to balance immediate gains with long-term vision. Sometimes, taking a job because it pays more makes sense. Other times, accepting a lower-paying role that stretches your skills and expands your network is the smarter move. Long-term thinkers aren't locked into one approach—they know how to play both sides. They can cash in when the moment is right while still building the foundation for their future.

The magic happens when you stop seeing your career as a series of isolated jobs and start viewing it as a body of work. Long game players don't chase titles for the sake of it—they chase impact. They think about how their work fits into a bigger picture and how every experience adds to their overall value. This perspective allows them to make intentional moves, even when the short-term payoff isn't obvious. They're willing to invest in themselves—whether that means learning a new skill, taking on tough projects, or building relationships—because they know those investments will pay dividends later.

And let's talk about patience—because the long game demands it. While others burn out chasing fast results, long-term thinkers stay steady. They understand that success is rarely immediate. It's a slow build that requires consistency, discipline, and resilience. There will be moments when it feels like nothing is happening—when the payoff isn't visible. This is when most people quit. But long-term thinkers know that real momentum takes time. They trust the process, even when the rewards aren't instant.

The long game mindset also gives you the ability to weather uncertainty. Industries evolve. Economies shift. Jobs disappear. But if you've been playing the long game—developing skills that transcend job descriptions and cultivating a strong professional network—you're adaptable. You aren't dependent on one company or one position to sustain you. Your value exists beyond a job title, which means you can pivot when necessary without losing traction. When you play the long game, you're never truly stuck.

Future-proofing your career isn't about predicting what's next—it's about preparing yourself to thrive no matter what happens. This means asking, "What skills will always be valuable, no matter how the world changes?" It means building relationships not because you need something today, but because you understand their value in the future. It means creating work that outlives the latest trend. Long-term thinkers aren't afraid of disruption—they're already preparing for what's coming next.

And here's the real win: the long game gives you leverage. When you've spent years building expertise, credibility, and relationships, you're no longer at the mercy of someone else's decisions. You can negotiate from a place of strength. You can walk away from roles that don't align with your goals. You become the person with options, and options equal power. While others are scrambling to keep up, you're deciding where you want to go next—because you've already laid the foundation.

Playing the long game also means thinking about your career legacy. What do you want to be known for? How do you want your work to impact the world? These questions guide long-term thinkers in ways that surface-level goals never could. It's not just about what you accomplish—it's about how those accomplishments shape the future. When you start thinking about legacy, you move differently. You focus on work that matters. You build things that last.

It's easy to be seduced by quick wins, but the real rewards go to those who play the long game. The people who quietly put in the work, stay consistent, and think beyond the immediate moment end up with careers that others envy. They aren't chasing opportunities—they're creating them. And while the short-term crowd is busy burning out, long-term thinkers are just getting started.

So, ask yourself: Are your current moves serving future you? Are you investing in skills and relationships that will still matter in a decade? Are you willing to be patient while the world chases the next quick fix? The long game isn't easy—but it's worth it. Because when you play the long game, you don't just survive the chaos—you shape it. And in the end, the people who think beyond this year are the ones who get to decide the future.

39

Bet on Yourself

AT SOME POINT, THE GRIND loses its shine. Titles blur together, paychecks start to feel routine, and even the most prestigious achievements fade into the noise. What lasts—what really leaves a mark—is the legacy you build. Legacy isn't just what you do while you're here; it's what continues when you're gone. It's the impact you leave behind—the work, ideas, and influence that shape others long after you've moved on. And while everyone else is busy chasing the next promotion, legacy-minded people are playing a different game. They're building something bigger than themselves.

Designing a career that outlasts your job means shifting your focus from immediate wins to long-term impact. Most people define success by external markers—title, salary, prestige—but those things are temporary. Legacy work is about what you create that others can build on. It's the systems you improve, the ideas you share, and the people you lift up along the way. When you start thinking in terms of legacy, your decisions shift. You're no longer just working for the next milestone—you're shaping a future where your influence continues, whether you're in the room or not.

One of the most powerful—and often overlooked—ways to leave a legacy is through mentorship. It's easy to focus on your own path, but the real magic happens when you extend a hand to others. Mentorship isn't just about sharing advice—it's about opening doors, offering insights, and helping someone else navigate spaces you've already crossed. And here's the thing: when you invest in others, you're also investing in yourself. Teaching forces you to refine your knowledge, strengthens your leadership skills, and expands your professional network in ways no solo hustle ever could.

The best mentors understand that legacy isn't about ego—it's about generosity. It's easy to guard your knowledge, to treat your expertise like a secret weapon. But hoarding wisdom is a short-term move. The people who truly shape industries are the ones who give freely. They don't just climb the ladder—they build new ones. And when you invest in others, your impact multiplies. The person you mentor today could go on to change the game tomorrow, and your fingerprints will be all over their success.

Beyond mentorship, legacy moves also mean building projects that outlast your involvement. Whether it's creating a new workflow, spearheading an initiative, or launching a community, the goal is to design something that keeps running even when you step away. This kind of work requires a different mindset— you're not just solving problems for now, but creating solutions that will serve future teams. It's about building with longevity in mind. And the best part? Legacy projects become proof of your vision. While others leave jobs with bullet points on a résumé, you leave behind structures that keep delivering value.

But let's be clear—legacy isn't about chasing glory. It's about purpose. Purpose-driven careers have staying power because they're rooted in something deeper than personal ambition. When your work aligns with what you care about, burnout becomes less likely. Purpose gives your career gravity—it keeps you grounded during chaotic seasons and motivated when the shine of external rewards fades. The people who play the long game know that success without significance is empty. They focus on work that matters because they understand that true power lies in what you give, not just what you take.

And here's the twist—legacy moves accelerate your professional growth. While everyone else is playing small and protecting their turf, you're operating on a larger scale. People who think about legacy get access to bigger opportunities because they're solving problems others can't see. When you're the person creating long-term value, decision-makers notice. You become the one people trust with major projects, the person they call when big moves need to be made. Legacy thinking gives you leverage—not just because of what you do, but because of the ripple effects it creates.

There's also a freedom that comes with legacy work. When you start playing for something bigger, you stop caring about petty office politics and short-term wins. You operate on a different frequency—one where your focus is on impact, not approval. Legacy thinkers don't get caught up in the noise because they're too busy shaping the future. And that mindset is rare. Most people are reacting to the present; you're building for what comes next. That difference gives you a level of clarity and influence that's hard to shake.

Another piece of legacy work? Sharing your knowledge openly. The most influential people aren't just doing the work—they're documenting and sharing it. Whether it's writing, speaking, or teaching, the act of sharing solidifies your expertise while creating a blueprint for others. You don't need a massive platform to start—what matters is putting your insights into the world. The things you've learned through hard-won experience? Someone else needs that knowledge. And when you share it, your legacy expands beyond your immediate circle.

Legacy isn't an accident—it's a choice. It requires intention. It means stepping beyond the day-to-day hustle to ask, *What am I really building?* It means being willing to invest in people and projects without an immediate return. It's about zooming out and realizing that the most meaningful careers are measured by impact, not just income. Legacy-minded people play the game differently because they aren't just chasing what's next—they're shaping what lasts.

And here's the truth: legacy moves aren't reserved for the people at the top. You don't need a fancy title or decades of experience to start building impact. Every decision you make— how you treat your colleagues, the systems you improve, the knowledge you share—contributes to the story you're writing. The question is, are you being intentional about what that story says? Because one day, you'll leave your current role. And when you do, the only thing that remains is the impact you made.

The people who leave the biggest marks on their industries aren't just the ones who worked the hardest. They're the ones who played for something bigger. They weren't obsessed with quick wins—they were building legacies. And while everyone else was busy chasing the next title, they were shaping futures. That's the difference. And it's a difference you can choose—starting now.

So, ask yourself: What are you building that will outlast you? Who are you investing in? What systems are you improving? Your career is temporary—but your legacy? That's forever. And if you're willing to play for something bigger, you'll create impact that echoes long after you've moved on.

40

You're Not Just a Worker

WELCOME TO THE AGE OF permanent career chaos—where job security is a relic of the past, industries shift overnight, and the only constant is change. If you're waiting for things to "settle down," you'll be waiting forever. The rules of work have been rewritten, and here's the truth: thriving in this new landscape isn't about avoiding uncertainty—it's about mastering it.

Chaos feels overwhelming because we're wired to crave stability. For decades, the career blueprint was simple—get a degree, land a steady job, and climb the corporate ladder. But that model is as outdated as dial-up internet. The future belongs to those who can flow with disruption rather than fear it. And the first step to thriving in career chaos is accepting that the mess isn't going anywhere. Once you stop resisting uncertainty, you can start using it to your advantage.

Think about it—uncertainty isn't just a threat; it's an opportunity factory. When the old systems crumble, there's room to build new ones. When industries evolve, new roles emerge. And when chaos hits, the most adaptable people rise. The people who cling to "how things used to be" will struggle. But the ones who see disruption as a playground for possibility? They're the ones who win. It's not about avoiding chaos—it's about building a career that can flex, stretch, and grow with it.

Building a career that adapts with you starts by ditching the idea that your identity is tied to one job, one company, or one industry. You are not your job title. You are a collection of skills, experiences, and ideas—assets that can be applied in multiple arenas. When you stop defining yourself by your current role, you unlock career fluidity. That means you're not stuck when things shift. You're ready to pivot, reimagine, and expand.

The key to this kind of career agility is skill stacking. Instead of clinging to one expertise, collect complementary skills that increase your versatility. A copywriter who understands SEO and data analytics is more valuable than one who doesn't. A marketer who knows how to code has more options than one who doesn't. Broadening your skill set doesn't just make you employable—it makes you unstoppable. And when the market shifts, you won't panic—you'll pivot.

But here's the catch—building an adaptive career isn't just about skills. It's about mindset. If you're operating from a place of fear, every disruption feels like a threat. But if you cultivate a mindset of curiosity and possibility, those same disruptions become doors to new opportunities. This shift—from survival to thriving—is what separates those who flourish in chaos from those who flounder.

Thriving in chaos also means redefining success. The old markers—corner offices, long tenures, gold watches—are irrelevant. Today, success looks like freedom, autonomy, and the ability to shape your own path. It's about creating a career that fits your life—not sacrificing your life to fit someone else's definition of success. When you focus on building a career that aligns with your values, you become more resilient because you're not chasing someone else's version of achievement.

And let's be honest—chaos isn't just external. The internal

game is just as important. If you're emotionally burned out or constantly second-guessing yourself, no amount of strategy will save you. That's why personal growth is the ultimate career asset. It's not just about what you know—it's about how you handle uncertainty, rejection, and change. People who prioritize emotional intelligence, self-compassion, and mental resilience have a superpower in chaotic times. They don't just survive the storm—they navigate it with clarity and strength.

This kind of internal work isn't glamorous, but it's non-negotiable. It means learning how to self-soothe when career anxiety spikes. It means staying grounded when everything around you is shifting. And it means trusting that your value isn't dependent on external validation. When you do this work, chaos loses its power to shake you. Because no matter how unpredictable the world becomes, you remain rooted in who you are and what you bring to the table.

Here's the other thing about chaos—it reveals who's really in control. In stable times, it's easy to coast. But when everything's upended, the people who take ownership of their careers stand out. Ownership means not waiting for your boss to map out your growth—it's building your own plan. It means treating your career like a business and making moves that serve your long-term vision. And it means rejecting the passive mindset that says, "I hope things work out" and embracing the active mindset of, "I'm making things happen."

Taking ownership also means protecting your energy. Career chaos is noisy—everyone's shouting about the next big thing, the latest trend, or the hottest opportunity. But not every opportunity is meant for you. The people who thrive long-term are the ones who know when to say no. They understand that every yes has a cost—so they choose intentionally. They set boundaries around their time and energy because they know that sustainability matters more than short-term hustle.

And let's talk about empowerment—because the ultimate flex in career chaos is staying empowered no matter what. Empowerment means understanding that while you can't control the external world, you always control your response. It's the difference between reacting and responding. When you react, you let circumstances dictate your emotions and actions. When you respond, you move with intention. You become the kind of person who doesn't crumble under uncertainty—you rise within it.

Empowerment also comes from building multiple streams of security. In chaotic times, a single paycheck is a fragile lifeline. That's why smart people are diversifying. Maybe that means a side hustle, freelance work, or passive income. Whatever the form, having multiple income streams gives you options. Options mean freedom. And freedom means you're not at the mercy of any one employer or industry.

The bottom line? Career chaos isn't going anywhere—but you have a choice. You can fight against the tide, hoping for a return to "normal," or you can embrace the mess and build a career that thrives within it. The world belongs to the adaptable. The question isn't whether chaos will continue—the question is whether you'll rise with it or get left behind.

So, stop waiting for things to stabilize. They won't. But here's the good news—you don't need stability to succeed. You need adaptability, ownership, and the courage to play your own game. And if you do? Career chaos won't break you—it'll make you unstoppable.